DATE DUE

OCT 3 0 1995	
APR - 8 1996	
MAR 1 4 1997	
APR 2 9 1997	
DEC - 1 1998	
MAR 3 0 1999	
JUL 2 0 2000	
AUG 0 8 2000	

BRODART, INC. | Cat. No. 23-221

FAITH, REASON, AND THE PLAGUE in Seventeenth-Century Tuscany

Also by Carlo M. Cipolla

Studi di Storia della Moneta (1948)
Mouvements Monétaires dans l'Etat de Milan (1951)
Verso il Far West (1952)
Money, Prices and Civilization in the Mediterranean World (1956)
Le Avventure della Lira (1958)
(Ed.) Storia dell'economia Italiana (1959)
The Economic History of World Population (1962)
Guns and Sails in the Early Phase of European Expansion (1965)
Clocks and Culture 1300–1700 (1967)
Literacy and Development in the West (1969)
(Ed.) The Economic Decline of Empires (1970)
(Ed.) The Fontana Economic History of Europe (1972–1976)
Cristofano and the Plague (1973)
Before the Industrial Revolution (1976)
Public Health and the Medical Profession in the Renaissance (1976)

FAITH, REASON, AND THE PLAGUE

in Seventeenth-Century Tuscany

CARLO M. CIPOLLA

Translated by Muriel Kittel

CORNELL UNIVERSITY PRESS
Ithaca, New York

First published 1979 by Cornell University Press

Library of Congress Cataloging in Publication Data
Cipolla, Carlo M
    Faith, reason, and the plague in seventeenth-century Tuscany.
    Translation of Chi ruppe i rastelli a Monte Lupo?
    Bibliography : p.
    1. Plague—Italy—Montelupo Fiorentino, 1630.
2. Public health—Italy—Montelupo Fiorentino—
History. 3. Montelupo Fiorentino, Italy—History—
17th century. I. Title.
RC178.19M66213 1979   614.5'73'2'094551   79–2479

ISBN 0-8014-1230-7

Printed by Bristol Typesetting Co. Ltd.,
and bound in Great Britain by
Redwood Burn Limited
Trowbridge and Esher

To Dante E. Zanetti,
Colleague and Friend

Contents

List of Figures

Preface

While working on the history of Public Health organization in Seventeenth century Italy I found myself reconstructing certain events which took place in Monte Lupo (Tuscany) during the epidemic of plague of 1630–31. Monte Lupo was in those days an insignificant village – so insignificant that I feel I ought to justify my decision to put the story in print.

There is always something of a storyteller in an historian and what happened in Monte Lupo in 1630–31 seemed to me such a good story that once I reconstructed it I could not resist the temptation of recounting it. But this is only part of the truth. So exceptionally rich is the documentation of Monte Lupo's story that it allows the historian to recapture emotions, attitudes, and behaviour of common people which all too often remain in the dark corners of history. Also what happened in that microcosm of Monte Lupo throws unexpected light on the relationship between Faith and Reason, Church and State at a social level where such problems rarely surface in historical documents. These considerations encouraged me to share my findings with the Public.

I just mentioned Faith and Reason, Church and State and the reader may wonder whether I am not indulging in modern stereotypes. Undoubtedly the Tuscans of the Seventeenth century did not see things in the way we do. To oversimplify an otherwise extremely complicated problem I would simply like to say that an important ingredient which specifically coloured the outlook of many Tuscans of the time was a widely diffused anti-clericalism which was not alternative to but coexisted with a deeply felt Faith. When in Monte Lupo's story some individuals opposed a rationalistic point of view to a religious one they did not think in terms of an abstract conflict between Reason and Faith. Faith was for them above discussion. But toward 'the priests' they nourished a peculiar mixture of scorn and hostility. With this caveat let me introduce Monte Lupo and its idiosyncratic inhabitants of 1630.

Acknowledgements

The research on which this book is based was largely supported by the National Institute of Health with grant 1 R01 LM 02324–01 from the National Library of Medicine. Additional financial support was provided by the Institute of International Studies at the University of California at Berkeley whose staff kindly and efficiently prepared the typescript.

I wish to extend my thanks to the above Institutions and to Muriel Kittel who translated the original Italian text capturing the spirit of the narrative with both competence and enthusiasm.

Appendix 1 is reprinted from *Cristofano and the Plague* by permission of the University of California Press, Berkeley and William Collins, Sons and Co. Limited, London.

C.M.C.

I

IN LATE Medieval and Renaissance Europe plague was endemic – and a constant nightmare. If they had to mention the dreaded word, most people would hasten to make the sign of the cross or to add the anxious invocation 'God deliver us from it'. When it flared up and took epidemic proportions as it did with dramatic frequency, the plague brought havoc and terror to cities and entire regions, killing in a very short time one quarter or one third of the population – or even more.

In the Christian West as in the Moslem East people thought of the plague as a Divine punishment, but, while in the Moslem East this belief contributed to the people's passive acceptance of the scourge, in the West it did not prevent society from taking active measures in the hope – or delusion – of limiting as far as humanly possible the extent of the disaster.

In Renaissance Italy some members of the clergy took a part in the fight against the plague. Especially the friars made a valuable contribution to the work of the health authorities, often braving conditions of unspeakable horror and nearly always at the risk of their lives; without their collaboration the health officials of the time would have found it practically impossible to operate the pesthouses in times of epidemics. We know the epic story of Father Antero Maria da San Bonaventura, who ran the pesthouse at Genoa during the epidemic of plague in 1657, because the Padre, although a victim of the disease himself, survived the terrifying experience and wrote an extraordinary book about it.[1] The story of Father Bisogni, who ran the pesthouse at San Miniato outside Florence during the epidemic of 1630, is practically unknown because the friar lost his life there, and only his sparse weekly reports to the Health Magistracy remain. There were also instances of ecclesiastics who were entrusted with high positions in health administration during epidemics. In Tuscany for example, during the epidemic of 1630 Nicolò Cini, canon of the Metropolitan Church, and Don Luca Mini, vicar of the Church of St. Stefano,[2] were appointed commissioners-general to supervise health affairs in the Florentine countryside. Their appointment had its own well-defined logic: in order to be effective in the countryside, the health authorities had necessarily to rely on the collaboration of the village priests, and the latter could be more easily handled by the high prelates of the metropolis than by the state bureaucracy. As for results, Canon Cini and Vicar Mini collaborated loyally with the health authorities.[3] All this is undeniable. But it is equally undeniable that the Health Magistracy and its representatives often met with strong and obstinate hostility from too many other members of the clergy. It was precisely in order to avoid such opposition that the Health Magistracy of Florence entrusted Canon Cini with another task that was more general and also much more delicate: 'the care of ecclesiastical matters in connexion with Public Health,' and specifically 'to see that both within and without the city of Florence the sick be administered the sacraments, and that members of the clergy observe the ordinances of the Health Authority for the public good.'[4]

'That members of the clergy observe the ordinances of

the Health Authority for the public good': this was one of the chief preoccupations of the health authority which was a powerful Magistracy, invested with 'absolute' powers but nevertheless severely limited by the ecclesiastical immunities – for while the Magistracy could proceed with requisitions, arrests, and sentences including the death penalty, against any lay person, whether noble or commoner, yet in cases of clergymen or ecclesiastical institutions the Magistracy encountered insurmountable difficulties, even in imposing a fine of a few pennies.

The Magistracy's concern over possible noncompliance or downright hostility from ecclesiastics with respect to health ordinances and officials was not unfounded. Particularly in times of epidemics, grounds for conflict between Public Health officials and men of the Church could appear at any moment, and in the most unexpected quarters. When conflicts developed between health and religious authorities, it was much easier to determine how the conflicts had originated than to predict how they could be resolved. The Health Commissioner for Volterra, the Florentine patrician, Luigi Capponi, who had to deal with the ill-tempered local Bishop, learned this lesson all too well. During the plague epidemic of 1630–3, the Commissioner had requested the Bishop to reduce the number of religious assemblies. The warning had aroused the Bishop's objections, which at first were restrained but later became quite vehement. The health measures were unpopular, and the Bishop had no trouble in winning local support for his cause. On 1 April 1632, Capponi wrote: 'Everyone is trying to create difficulties because they are annoyed by my presence,' and apropos the Bishop, he added bluntly: 'He can excommunicate me or do whatever he pleases; I do not care; I am here only to serve His

Serene Highness.' The conflict between the two became progressively more bitter and was encouraged by the local petty nobility who thoroughly enjoyed the chance to annoy a Florentine patrician. Hoping to get rid of Capponi, the Bishop appealed to Secretary of State Cioli, but realizing that he was not getting his way he gathered witnesses and evidence to prove that (a) Capponi had told his assistants that he had the authority to arrest people in church even if they were kneeling; (b) Capponi's guards had chased people into church, causing public scandal; (c) on the first Sunday of March Capponi's guards had molested people who were taking part in a procession; (d) they had gone as far as to arrest the crossbearer without the Bishop's authorization; and (e) the Commissioner had been so strict in isolating the infected monasteries that the cloistered nuns of Santa Chiara had been forced to come right up to their windows and call on people in the street to supply the things they needed, thus creating another public scandal. The Bishop concluded his charges by adding that Commissioner Capponi was also a heretic, because he had reproved a number of citizens for 'believing more in priests than in the Lord himself'.

The case against the Commissioner had been set up in secret at the Bishop's court by the Bishop's vicar, and the witnesses were nearly all priests and nuns. When the proceedings were then transmitted to the Grand Duke so that he could take the necessary measures, the Grand Duke handed over the thorny matter to his own magistrates, who were members of the same social class as Capponi. The magistrates studied the proceedings point by point and reached conclusions which could not have pleased the Bishop in the least. First of all, the Florentine magistrates pointed out that the allegations had been

4

gathered 'in a passionate manner, without the guarantee of notaries and chancellors and that the witnesses had been questioned in a suggestive fashion.' As far as individual accusations were concerned, the magistrates pointed out that the crossbearer (the sacristan, Leoni) was not a cleric, and consequently his arrest was perfectly legal. With regard to the lamentable affair of the convent of Santa Chiara, the magistrates pointed out that Capponi had earlier obtained the Bishop's permission to place guards there, and that the nuns had always had all their needs met: if the nuns had come to the windows to talk to people in the street they had done so 'without any necessity'. As far as the Commissioner's heresy was concerned, it was altogether nonexistent, 'since reproaching those who believe more in a priest than in God is certainly not a crime, but rather a just reproach, and, furthermore, the issue did not involve articles of faith but violations of health ordinances.' The Grand Duke's magistrates concluded, therefore, that Commissioner Capponi had always acted in the interests of Public Health and in the service of His Serene Highness and not as the Bishop asserted 'to prove his own superiority to ecclesiastical authority'. As a final touch, the magistrates gave the Bishop some of his own medicine, pointing out that the episcopal trial was 'the result of passion and maliciousness and not an attempt to safeguard ecclesiastical immunity and jurisdiction'.[5] In this manner the Florentine aristocracy, which was at one with the high bureaucracy of the state, united against the interferences of the ecclesiastical bureaucracy – and this despite the accommodating character of the Grand Duke Ferdinand II (1621–1670) who had no desire to tangle with Rome.

Conflicts between the health authorities and the men

of the Church were an everyday occurrence in times of epidemics, and were certainly not limited to the higher circles of the two bureaucracies. The hostility was also apparent at lower levels, and unfortunately when the conflicts occurred there the health authority's guards occasionally behaved with a brutality that was embarrassing to the magistracy. A young countryman went to Pistoia to make some purchases, and when he presented his health pass at the city gate, a health guard tore up the pass shouting, 'This is how we should handle people whose priests speak ill of the Magistracy of Health.'[6] On another occasion when a friar came to enter a city gate a health guard hit him across the buttocks with a halberd, and shouted, 'Be off, be off you slobbering monk!' At the height of exasperation with the continuous protests and complaints from bishops, abbots, vicars, and curates, the Pope – an irascible Barberini – decided to excommunicate all Magistrates of Public Health in Florence.[7]

The most frequent sources of conflict between clergymen and health officers were: the quarantine measures to which the clergy were not always willing to submit; the requisition of monasteries or other religious premises which the officers needed to transform into temporary pesthouses or places for convalescents; and last, but not least, the sermons and processions. During epidemics the health officers did not look favourably upon gatherings of people. As a Florentine ordinance of 1533 put it, 'they have had the experience that assemblies and gatherings of people in times of contagion have the worst consequences.'[8] Therefore when they felt that the disease was reaching or had already reached epidemic proportions, the Health Magistracy moved swiftly to order the closing of schools,[9] the suspension of popular games,[10] the banning

6

of parties and dances and so forth. As far as sermons and processions were concerned, there is no doubt that most of the health officers shared the religious convictions of their time, and felt that the sermons and processions might appease God, and thus perhaps help to bring the epidemic to an end. But while the appeasement of God's wrath through sermons and processions appeared to the health officers as a possibility, the exacerbation of contagion through large assemblies of people was for them a certainty. It is significant that at this period – the period of the Scientific Revolution – the Health Magistrates generally decided in favour of the teaching of 'experience' rather than that of faith, in spite of their religious convictions, and doubtless at the expense of inner conflicts. But they were few in number, fighting against the many who preferred to believe rather than observe. The many were guided by the men of the Church, and with very few exceptions[11] the men of the Church had not the slightest doubt: processions and similar ceremonies were the only way to placate divine wrath and put an end to the scourge.

In November, 1630, while the plague was still raging in Florence, the Prior of the Monastery of St. Marco was unable to rest. According to his own testimony the good Prior was tormented 'day and night', brooding over the thoughts that the 'severe scourge' had been sent by the Almighty 'from the treasury of His wrath', and that the persistence of the epidemic was the result of the 'blindness of men who think they can remedy this loss of life that is sent from Heaven, solely with human care *contra consilium Altissimi* [contrary to the Almighty's purpose].' The Prior did not for a moment suspect the role played by bacilli, rats, and fleas – but neither did the health

7

officials. Both parties thought along erroneous and yet clearly divergent lines. For the Prior, God's anger was at the root of the disaster. For the health officials, the cause might well have been God's anger, but it was also and above all the 'miasmas', the 'vapours', the 'contagiousness' of the disease, no matter how this cursed 'contagiousness' operated.

The difference between the two positions was not the difference between truth and error, but between two kinds of error – one blindly rooted in ideology, the other derived from inadequate means of observation. The ideologue poured scorn on the empiricist: 'The blindness of men who think they can remedy this loss of life that is sent from Heaven solely with human care and contrary to the Almighty's purpose.' The strength of the theologian lay solely in his own obtuse blindness. On the other hand the pragmatists were tormented by the complexity of 'experience', and by their inner religious doubts which played into the hands of their opponents. Apart from these and other psychological factors, the Prior of St. Marco was a man of consequence in the Florence of his day; and he would not keep quiet. After writing to the Grand Duke that the Florentines' 'blindness' gave him insomnia, he wrote to Andrea Cioli, First Secretary of State, proclaiming that he 'lamented the plague and feared the worst, suspecting that the city's silence towards God displeased Him'; and since he had to pontificate in Latin, he added his fear that the Lord *tezaurizet nobis iram in haec die ire* [would concentrate His anger on us in this day of wrath].' The sleepless Prior managed to stir up enough action that with the support of the new Archbishop he was eventually able to organize a procession – making, however, one great concession to the health authority:

8

namely, that the only participants in this procession, besides a chosen number of clergy, were to be the Grand Duke and his court and the Senators in their purple – to the total exclusion of the populace. In order to keep the latter at a distance 'at a very early hour in the morning all corners of the neighbouring streets were occupied by horse guards and sergeants so that nobody might pass.' But even this was not enough to allay the fears of the health officials who, as an extra precaution, had the streets strewn with 'fragrant herbs'. And while the health officers held their breath, the people were happy to watch the magnificent procession from their doorways, with lighted torches in their hands; and a nun wrote that on that very same day (5 December 1630), 'St. Antonio, whose remains were borne gloriously through the city, cured 400 people sick of the plague.'[12]

II

DURING THE fifteenth and sixteenth centuries the major
states of central northern Italy – specifically: Venice,
Milan, Genoa, and Florence – had developed a detailed
organization of public health far in advance of the rest
of Europe.[1] This system took the form of a series of institutions and regulations that would later be used as models
by various other European states and communities. These
ideas, institutions, and laws that were developed in the
fifteenth and sixteenth centuries and reached maturity in
the seventeenth, naturally suffered from the medical and
scientific ignorance of the period. The health officials were
anxious to fight the recurrent epidemics of 'plague' – but
what exactly constituted the plague was unknown, and
a disease was often called the plague when it was not.
Above all, there were no correct ideas concerning the
etiology of disease: neither the pathogen nor its vectors
were identified, and it was not known how illness spread
and became epidemic.

Ignorance of the pathogen and of the mechanisms of
propagation of the disease meant that preventive measures
were little better than shots in the dark. People were
groping blindly then as we are now in our search for ways
to stop the spread of neoplasms. And working in the dark
leads to errors, wasted resources, and the accusation of
innocents. Some of the ordinances were actually counter-
productive, such as the orders for the mass slaughter of

dogs and cats, in the belief that the coats of those animals harboured the plague-bearing miasma; nobody even dimly suspected that killing all those poor animals made life easier for the rats which were the real source of disease. Other ordinances were unnecessarily severe, such as the imposition of a 22-day quarantine on those exposed to contagion, whereas today a quarantine of six or seven days is regarded as adequate.

On the other hand, repeated observation had suggested some valid ideas which gave rise to ordinances, the wisdom of which nobody now would think of questioning. These were ordinances requiring, under severe penalties, that cases of illness be promptly reported, that the sick person be immediately isolated, that all those exposed to disease be kept under observation, that during epidemics schools be closed and assemblies avoided, that the bedding and clothes of persons dead of the plague be burned, and so on.

I have reproduced in Appendix 1 the 'Instructions of the Magistracy of Health in Florence to the Ministers of Justice Outside the City in Cases of Sickness from the Plague Found Within Their Jurisdiction, Particularly in the Country Districts and Villages'. In the cities a more complex set of regulations was in force, but because the story we have to tell took place in a rural area, the text of the 'Instructions' is more pertinent to the matter at hand. The curious reader who is willing to take the trouble to look at these instructions will get a direct impression of what health legislation was like at that time, i.e. a strange mixture of brilliant intuition, sound common sense, and absurd prejudice.

Even when the health ordinances were wise, they met

with strong opposition. At best they were a source of great annoyance to most people; in the majority of cases they caused great misery and severe privations. The segregation of entire families in their homes, the separation of kindred in the horror of the pesthouses, the closing of markets and trade, the consequent lack of work and widespread unemployment, the burning of furnishings and goods – all were unpopular provisions, to say the least. The doctor in Busto Arsizio who was bold enough to report the presence of plague in his town in 1630 and by implication requested quarantine controls, brought arquebus fire on himself and lost his life. Doctors Settala and Tadino in Milan escaped that end, but their carriages were stoned by the mob when they had to pass through the poor sections of the city. Ignorance and penury were the main causes of infraction of the rules. Gravediggers trafficked in the clothes of the dead; carriers exchanged or forged health passes; innkeepers ignored the controls. But the lower classes were not the only offenders. The merchants put every obstacle they could in the way of health inspections, limitations on trade, and the quarantines. The well-to-do classes opposed the imposition of extra taxes to defray the costs of health administration. Others considered that restriction of their movements was intolerable, and guards at the gates were constantly being insulted by all sorts of people and worked out their frustrations by abusing the poor. The clergy, as we have seen, did not readily adapt themselves to the limitations placed by health authorities on processions and other large religious functions, while bishops and monks ill supported the requisitioning of their churches and monasteries for use as hospitals. Even nobler feelings could lead to infractions: it was not easy to report the illness of a parent, child, or brother, and then to see them carried away and locked up in the dreadful charnel-houses called *lazaretti*. Thus, ignorance, egoism, avarice, and bullying joined with family ties and religious feeling to impede and negate the work of the health authorities, and to encourage the lethal operation of the microbes.

In general, the implementation of the rules depended less on consent than on the presence of a police force that could ensure the observance of the regulations in question. For this reason the situation in smaller and more isolated communities was worse than in the larger cities.

III

At Monte Lupo matters were no better than elsewhere – in fact, they were considerably worse.

Monte Lupo was a small walled village of the type known in Tuscany as a *castello,* situated about thirty kilometres from Florence; it was perched on a low hill overlooking both the road to Pisa and the River Arno at the gorge of Golfolina. As the author of the *Viaggio Pittorico della Toscana* wrote in 1801: 'History makes no mention of anything important happening in this castello since 1249', the date of a great battle,[1] and as far as the castello's appearance was concerned 'there is nothing there of any interest to the Fine Arts or their history, while most of the buildings are rustic and rather crude and uncouth in taste.'[2]

At the beginning of the seventeenth century some 150 families must have been living within the castello's walls.[3] A large majority of them were very poor and they were a difficult sort. 'In this castello are a type of people who fear neither God nor Justice, and in all the territory of our most Serene Lord [i.e. the Grand Duke] there is no worse a populace, and they are well known for this.' That was written in 1631 by Father Giovanni Dragoni, Dominican monk and Vicar of St. Niccolò in Monte Lupo, and it was not just an old man's grumbling. At about the same time, Francesco della Stufa, mayor of Monte Lupo, reported to Florence that the people of Monte Lupo were of such a nature that 'they would not be held in check.' And Michelagniolo Coveri, a surgeon for the Health Magistracy of Florence who had had to deal with the Monte Lupans, dared not go near the castello without an arquebus, 'fearing that he would be attacked in passing through that place.'[4]

The plague appeared in Tuscany in August 1630, and before the end of September had already struck Monte Lupo. It reached there before most of the other Tuscan centres and lasted relatively longer. The fact that the plague arrived in Monte Lupo earlier than elsewhere cannot be attributed to the inhabitants – unless we suppose that the Lord was particularly unhappy with them because of their difficult character. But the fact that the contagion lasted longer and caused greater losses in Monte Lupo must bear a certain relationship to the poverty and nature of the people.

According to concordant evidence from a report from the neighbouring town of Empoli and from the parish book of the dead in the castello, the disease began in the inn outside the gate. On 1 September, Maddalena Mostardini died at the inn. On 16 September, Andrea, the twelve-year-old son of the innkeeper also died at the inn. Between 28 September and 1 October Aurelio Mostardini, the innkeeper lost a sister-in-law, a daughter, and, finally, his wife. The inn seemed to be under a curse – and the evil did not stop there. On 4 October, there occurred the death of Master Mazzuoli's wife, who, according to the Empoli report had 'frequented' the inn but lived inside the castello walls.[5] The epidemic was obviously spreading (cf. Fig. 3). Already alarmed, the

16

neighbouring communities quickly took the necessary precautions. Pistoia, Empoli, and other centres closed their gates to the Monte Lupans, and the Health Magistracy of Florence ordered the isolation of the castello. A stockade was erected in front of the main gate and Monte Lupo was cut off.

Father Giovanni Dragoni, a Dominican, was vicar of the priory at St. Niccolò. A man in his sixties, he was the most prominent and best educated person in Monte Lupo. Not that one had to have much learning to shine in Monte Lupo, even though the village boasted two school-teachers,[6] but the cultural difference encouraged a certain distinction. The Father's opinion of the castello's inhabitants has already been quoted. Father Dragoni was not an easygoing man: he had a high opinion of himself, without a trace of humility, which made him hypercritical of others. He grumbled continually and did not mince matters in his criticisms; he also had idiosyncrasies, such as considering card games to be inventions of the Devil. Nonetheless he had very considerable gifts: he was deeply honest, a clear thinker, still vigorous of pulse despite his age, and endowed with great practical sense. The combination of these qualities made Father Dragoni an excellent administrator.[7]

When the plague first appeared in Monte Lupo, he was the first to notify the health authority in Florence (an act which certainly did not make him more popular with the villagers), and as he 'kept a few supplies' at the priory, it was he who furnished first aid, distributing 'antidotes, theriac, ceric, and other things, for the love of God', before help arrived from Florence.[8] The Florentine Health

Magistrates had a high opinion of the Father and gave clear and early evidence of their esteem when in the first days of the epidemic, they appointed him Head and Bursar of Public Health in Monte Lupo.

In the castello, as was usual in such circumstances, there was provision for electing 'Deputies of Public Health' from among the local people. In the cities and in villages of a certain size there were people of rank – 'gentlemen' – from among whom deputies could be chosen and appointed. But in Monte Lupo there were no 'gentlemen', and even illiterates were elected deputies.[9] This made Father Dragoni's role even more important, and in any case his position as Head conferred on him full authority over his colleagues. As the castello was closed off and in the grip of the epidemic this appointment gave him almost dictatorial power over life in the village. But controlling the people of Monte Lupo was an impossible task, even for a man of Father Dragoni's calibre.

In order to bury those dead of the plague a special cemetery was established in open country away from the village in the neighbourhood of Cacciacane, between Monte Lupo and San Miniatello (cf. Fig. 1); to isolate the sick a pesthouse was opened, also outside the town in the direction of San Miniatello, in a place called 'the tall house'.[10] According to the notes made by the parish priest, Bontadi, the pesthouse was opened on 11 October, and, from papers in the Public Health Archives, we know that eight days later, i.e. on the 19th, a surgeon, Fortunato di Orazio Folli, arrived from Florence with orders from the Health Magistracy to take up his duties at the hospital.[11] There were eight patients at the beginning, but their

18

number rapidly increased so that by 22 October there were 28 sick men and women in the pesthouse.[12] According to the Instructions of the Health Magistracy in Florence (cf. Appendix 1), the relatives of the dead and of those admitted to the pesthouse were quarantined in their houses, and it was obviously necessary to provide them with food. Money, however, was lacking. The cost of distributing bread to the sick in the pesthouse and to those quarantined at home amounted to more than five *scudi* a day by the middle of November, and by 16 December the Health Deputies had incurred a debt of 44 *scudi* 'on account of said bread'. Up until 19 December, the surgeon, Folli, after serving in the pesthouse for almost two months, had received nothing beyond the five *scudi* paid him in advance by the Health Magistracy in Florence when he took up his duties. A subsidy of 22 *scudi* did arrive from Florence on 19 December, but it was only a drop in the bucket compared with the unpaid debts and the continuously growing expenses. It was clearly necessary to resort to extraordinary fiscal measures. But to impose taxes on those people of Monte Lupo was not easy, and trouble began.[13]

There were good reasons for this. Most of the people were poor, and the isolation of the castello had intensified the general and already great wretchedness. For the majority to pay any additional tax was almost impossible. But, in addition, those who could pay offered resistance: in fact, they were worse than the others. Alessandro Bartoletti spread the rumour that the health authority in Florence had sent a subsidy of 200 *scudi,* and went around encouraging his peasants and others not to pay. People willingly listen to what they want to hear, and resistance went beyond all bounds. Even Aurelio Mostardini, the innkeeper outside the wall, refused to pay the extra tax, and to Father Dragoni, whose temper was exacerbated by all this 'disorder', this was intolerable. 'From his house have been carried out six corpses dead of the plague,' wrote the Father angrily, 'and he should be made to burn all the bedding and utensils because he brought the disease into Monte Lupo.'[14]

But to command obedience in Monte Lupo required more than persuasion or reason. Force was necessary, and force was not at Father Dragoni's disposal – or at least not in an adequate form: 'The beadle cannot act alone. Our messenger is a wretched old man who can hardly move.' The energetic Father asked Florence for help: he requested to be sent two guards because, he wrote, 'I cannot carry out my duty without the stronger arm of the law.'[15]

The need for guards in Monte Lupo was very real, and not only to execute the health ordinances and collect taxes. Profiting from a situation where many were locked up in the pesthouse, and where entire families were confined to their homes and nobody was allowed to move around at night, certain scoundrels began to rob the houses. Thieves entered the house of Costantino Berti and carried off two gold rings, a pearl and garnet necklace, as well as clothes and woollen cloth. Sandra di Boba's house was robbed while the poor woman was in the hospital: the thieves took millet and two shirts. There were no people in Paola della Mencona's house because they had all died of the plague, but it was full of good things. The thieves forced the bars erected by the health authority and emptied the house as well. They robbed the innkeeper

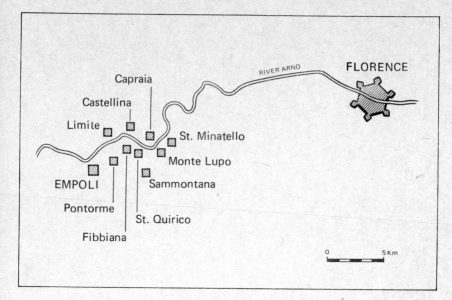

Fig. 1   PLACES MENTIONED IN THIS BOOK

On the map: for Firenze read Florence
for S. Miniatello read St. Miniatello
for S. Quirico read St. Quirico

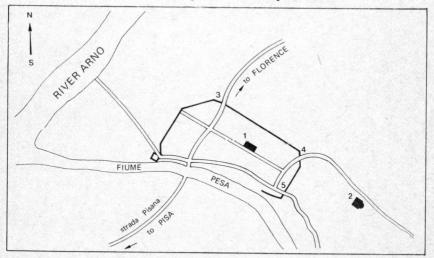

Fig. 2:   MONTE LUPO:

1. Church and Convent of St. Niccolò
2. Church of St. Giovanni Evangelista
3. The St. Miniatello gate
4. The pear tree gate
5. The olive tree gate

In 1784 the church of St. Giovanni had its name changed into that
of St. Lorenzo and the church of St. Niccolò had its name changed
into that of St. Giovanni

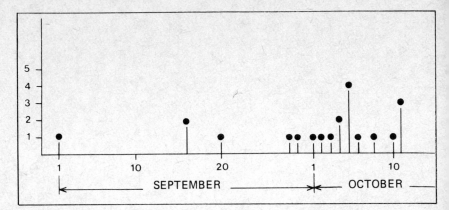

Fig. 3 Daily number of deaths in Monte Lupo between 1 September and 11 October 1630 according to the parish books of the deceased

GRATIS.

Adi 10 di ... 1630.

Noi infrascritti Deputati à fare le presenti bullette d'ordine de SS. Offiziali di Sanità della Città di Firenze facciamo fede con giuramento, à chiunque s'aspetta come parte di ...

Sano della sua persona, & il quale nella Casa doue habita non ha hauuto, ne ha Ammalati di sospetto d'alcuna sorte, che così siamo certificati per leggitimi riscontri, e giustificationi &c.

Di Anni

Pelo

Statura

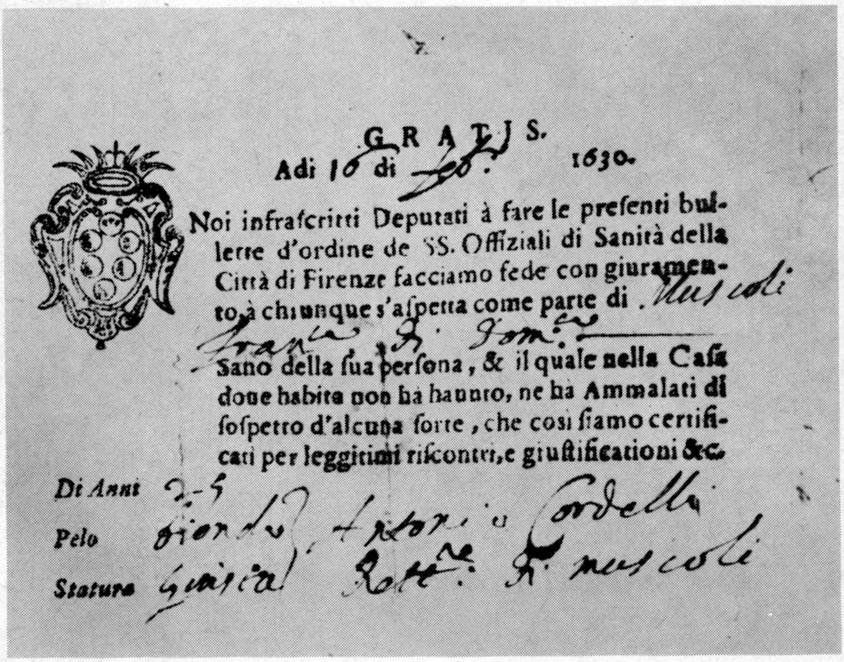

Fig. 4 A printed health-pass of the type used in Tuscany in 1630-1

outside the gate of oil, cheese, hemp, and other goods from one of his storehouses. An attempted break-in took place at Onofrio Gigli's home, but the door was too stout. While trying to force entry into Alessandro Coppiardi's house, the thieves took down the door props, but the noise woke the inmates and the thieves were put to flight. They also tried to rob Agniolo Forzini, the miller; with the help of a ladder, the thieves reached a window of the house and tried to prise off the bolt, with a saddlemaker's needle. The people inside the house were quarantined on account of the plague. The miller was sleeping heavily and heard nothing, but the noise woke an old woman who began to scream. Realizing that they were discovered, the thieves fled, abandoning both the ladder and the needle. Next day, the ladder was recognized as belonging to Sandro di Bastiano Mazzuoli, from whom it had been stolen the day before. The needle, however, turned out to be a valuable clue: it was identified as the property of Raffaello Bonecchi, known as *Il Macchia* (the Spot), a mattress-maker. Notified of these misdeeds, the Constable of Florence, Captain Piero da Pontassieve, sent two of his men to Monte Lupo, and *Il Macchia* was arrested. *Il Macchia* then revealed the name of an accomplice, one Francesco di Giovan Battista Bartoloni, known as *Il Romano* (the Roman), who was also arrested. The culprits confessed their thefts; among other things it emerged that *Il Macchia* had also broken into his mother-in-law's cottage, and carried off more articles.[16]

The action of the Constable and his men had been swift and effective, but police action was insufficient to stop the disintegration of social life in Monte Lupo. Conflicts of jurisdiction increased the confusion. As it happened, a Commissioner from the Health Magistracy in Florence and a newly appointed Mayor had arrived in the castello, bringing with them contradictory orders. On 10 January, Father Dragoni complained to Florence: 'One orders one thing, and the other another, and between them they are so contradictory that I don't know whom to obey. Your Health Commissioner leaves me an order and His Honour the Mayor appears and gives another completely opposite, and they both swear they have authority.' For a man who liked clarity, the situation was anything but pleasant – but this was not all. The new Mayor seems at first to have opposed Father Dragoni's strictness, and the Father grumbled in his letter that 'in the end my hands have been tied.' In that nest of vipers which was Monte Lupo the inhabitants took advantage of these conflicts, and as Father Dragoni reported: 'The opposition are encouraged to mock me and the health deputies, and to spread the rumour that I have no authority, and they have told me to my face that I should attend to my church.' Father Dragoni came to the logical conclusion: 'if strictness is not to be observed, and if the orders I have issued are to be cancelled, I resign my commission.'[17] The Florentine magistrates, however, had full confidence in him, and hastened to write to him on 15 January that 'if orders have sometimes come that contradict each other, it is not our Magistracy's intention to diminish your authority.'[18] Father Dragoni no longer spoke of resigning, and the episode was closed, but the basic problem remained. As the Father reported, 'Monte Lupo has become another Babylon. The greater God's punishments are, the more wicked people become. We have here larceny, gambling dens, and card games.'[19] By general rule, the gravediggers

22

were supposed to remain isolated in their houses when they were not working, because their continual contact with bodies dead of the plague made them suspect as possible carriers of infection. Any infraction of this rule was considered serious, but the two gravediggers of Monte Lupo 'have transgressed the edicts and ordinances, and have gone about Monte Lupo day and night, bearing arms.' As if this were not bad enough, one of them 'with a stick broke the head of a poor fellow' with whom he had quarrelled.[20] Father Dragoni had him locked up, but what could be done with such rascals? 'There are no guards here,' lamented the Father in one letter, and in another he asked for instructions and advice on 'how to proceed against transgressors of the edicts and ordinances, and against the gamblers and other delinquents when there are no guards. Here is fear of neither God nor Justice.'[21]

In January the Health Magistracy decided to impose a general quarantine on the entire state. This meant confining the whole population to their houses for at least forty days – the healthy along with the sick and those suspected of infection – under the pious illusion that by reducing social contacts to a minimum the epidemic would be given its *coup de grâce*. The decision to impose a general quarantine was taken when it seemed that the epidemic was in a declining phase. Rats and fleas were obviously ignored because no one suspected their role in spreading contagion. Today, with this knowledge, no epidemiologist would look favourably on a general quarantine that shut people up in houses harbouring the source of infection. However, the people of the time rebelled at the idea of a general quarantine not because of scientific principles but because such a measure meant the almost total cessation of economic activity, and therefore a greater degree of misery when the prevailing levels of poverty were already intolerably high.

The order to put the general quarantine into effect was brought to Father Dragoni soon after the middle of January by Michelagniolo Coveri, the surgeon. On 18 January Father Dragoni wrote to Florence acknowledging the order and asking for detailed instructions: could the women leave their homes for provisions, had the quarantine to be applied to the castello alone or to the whole district, could the health officers hold their meetings during the quarantine.[22] His meticulousness compelled him to ask these questions, but at the same time his innate common sense caused him to write an additional memorandum which he entrusted to Coveri and in which he explained the difficulties in effecting a quarantine in the castello. Four days later, on 22 January he wrote again to Florence saying that he had not begun the quarantine, and that he was 'in great confusion' because he had not yet received answers either to his memorandum or to his questions. And he tenaciously reiterated his point of view: 'There is no possibility here of carrying out the quarantine. I saw with my own eyes crowds of poor wretches gathering all kinds of weeds that one would not even give to animals, and if they do find enough, they feed themselves on these without any condiment, not even a bit of salt.' Father Dragoni wrote of these things because his conscience directed him to do so. But his conscience was also that of a law-abiding man, and thus he added: 'Nevertheless, if your lordships wish the quarantine to be effected, I shall, as your minister, have it carried out according to your least instructions.' But then the other part of his conscience took control, and the letter continued: 'The Lord God does not desire the death of the poor, and I am more than certain that neither do your lordships intend it.'[23]

This close sequence of contradictory statements in the same letter reveals the drama of a person who was fundamentally human and honest, but at the same time strictly faithful to the law. The law is an abstraction based on general categories, while reality takes many forms and is made up of an extreme variety of individual cases. The literal application of the law can mean great wrong to the individual; evading the law to save the single case can mean opening the dike to the flood of social chaos. Demagogues and tyrants find their solution through arbitrary action. Father Dragoni was neither tyrant nor demagogue. He notified the legislators of the harshness of the law, but, however harsh and unfair he considered it, the law still remained the law for him, and as such he was ever ready to uphold and impose it. On the other hand, the people identified the monk with a law they did not understand, and saw him only as the hated and feared representative of a distant authority, if not a quite intolerable dictator who arrogated unjustified authority and rights to himself: 'They have spread the rumour that the commissions and letters of your lordships are my inventions.'[24] Loneliness is the price a man has to pay when in a position of ultimate responsibility: Father Dragoni did not mind the loneliness but he resented the hostility and the malice which surrounded him in the Castello.

As a contemporary report stated, Monte Lupo 'had suffered great onslaughts of the plague,'[25] and a petition from the community dated 22 January noted that only 135 families were left in the castello.[26] The poverty was extreme: according to the petition only twenty families were not in a condition of total indigence. The bread eaten in the village was disgusting because it was made of everything but grain.[27] Precisely because of the castello's poverty-stricken state, the Health Magistracy in Florence had agreed that the quarantine be mildly enforced in Monte Lupo: that people should only be prevented 'from going from one house to another, and that assemblies be prohibited; otherwise . . . they should be allowed to go about their business.'[28] The Magistracy's leniency was a relief for the Monte Lupans. Further relief was afforded by the fact that the epidemic seemed definitely to be nearing its close: on 11 February, Father Dragoni reported that 'today there are no more sick in the pesthouse at Monte Lupo',[29] and ten days later, following his inspection of the castello, Commissioner Gondi wrote to Florence that 'in Monte Lupo the disease has almost died out.'[30] The winter's cold had evidently stopped the epidemic. The pesthouse was closed, and to complete the return to normality only the revocation of the edict isolating Monte Lupo was needed from Florence; but this was no light matter. In such cases the Florentine Health Magistracy acted with understandable prudence and circumspection. By 13 March Monte Lupo was still cut off, and Father Dragoni reported that 'these people of Monte Lupo rebel against me, thinking that I am the one who prevents their free passage. . . . At present they are on the point of coming here in crowds to make an appeal to your lordships.'[31]

Father Dragoni was always well informed about what was going on in the village, and his prediction was punctually fulfilled. On 14 March the Monte Lupans went 'in crowds' to the town hall and requested that Father Dragoni and his colleagues the health deputies send a petition to Florence.[32] The request was not absurd, and five days later the health authority in Florence decided to allow free movement and commerce to the Monte Lupans provided that any person leaving the castello carried the proper health pass certifying the good health of the pass-holder. The passes – it was clearly specified – 'shall be issued by Father Giovanni Dragoni.'[33] The monk wrote back to Florence on Tuesday 25 March 'in the name of all the deputies,' thanking the Magistracy for their decision; as for the 'responsiblity for the passes,' the Father declared that 'I accept this for the present, in order to obey all your lordships' orders.'[34] Father Dragoni obeyed, but he was very tired of having to deal with the Monte Lupans. He had never wanted power for its own sake. He had accepted the appointment out of a sense of duty and obedience, and, as he himself complained, 'In reward for this I have suffered great vexations.'[35] Now that the epidemic was over and all seemed in order, his only desire was to return to the peace and seclusion of his monastery. Tactfully he contacted Commissioner Gondi and requested to be relieved of his office. Meanwhile he continued to be vigilant and to fulfil his duties with his customary diligence. The Health Magistracy had decided to allow the people of Monte Lupo to go to Florence on business, provided that they were furnished with health passes, but the Magistracy had not yet arranged to send the printed forms to the Castello. Father Dragoni was therefore obliged to issue passes written entirely by hand on any odd pieces of paper. The Monte Lupans quickly took advantage of this to make false passports, forging the Father's signature. Hearing of these new misdeeds, Father Dragoni wrote hastily and in great alarm on 27 March to warn the Magistracy. He did not entrust the letter to the usual messenger but sent one of the health deputies to Florence. The Father enclosed in the letter a fascimile of the handwritten passes he was issuing (Fig. 5) to enable the Magistracy and the guards to check the validity of the passes that were presented by the Monte Lupans at the gates in Florence.[36]

It seemed as if Father Dragoni's tribulations would never come to an end, but a communication arrived at that very time which must have given him both relief and satisfaction. Commissioner Gondi had transmitted his request to Florence to be excused from his duties, and the answer was favourable. The Health Magistracy was aware of the outstanding manner in which Father Dragoni had conducted himself, and also of the resentment and malevolence his strict administrative methods had aroused against him; the magistrates not only accepted his request but sent him a letter of high praise as well.[37] With no delay, Father Dragoni left the cares of the Health Board and returned to the peace of his convent.

To act as deputies for the health authority among the uncouth and rebellious people of Monte Lupo could not have been easy even for educated and energetic men. For those who held office in the Castello it was virtually impossible: one of them was illiterate, and to judge from their handwriting the others were barely literate.

The letter in which the Magistracy in Florence accepted Father Dragoni's resignation was written on 28 March. Scarcely four days elapsed before the deputies of Monte

Lupo wrote to Florence saying that they had 'heard' of the Magistracy's decision and were 'amazed' at the Father's resignation. Why did he not wish to remain at his post 'to win reward from the Almighty and honour from the world?' They were utterly distressed: 'At the peak of the contagion the Father had proved himself so well personally and by his intelligence that no harm nor any disturbance arose between us deputies and others, and we have always obeyed and agreed to his commands because we saw that they were true and just.' Now that the Father was leaving, what on earth were they to do left to themselves? 'Not having the aforementioned Father as Head and leader we beg for leave.'[38] The reply came quickly – but it was not what the deputies were hoping for: on 4 April the Health Magistracy wrote back in rather harsh terms reminding the deputies 'of their duty to the state' and ordering them 'to continue their office'.[39]

It is not difficult to imagine the disappointment of the poor deputies. To make things worse, the plague had not disappeared among the rats of Monte Lupo, and, if the fleas had either died or hibernated during the cold winter months, they began to proliferate again with the coming of spring – thus reactivating the epizootic that in turn reactivated the epidemic. To their dismay, the helpless deputies of Monte Lupo soon found themselves confronted with a new wave of plague. On 18 April 1631 the Magistracy in Florence sent the surgeon, Domenico Corsi 'to visit that place and to give the necessary orders'; five days later, on the basis of the surgeon's report, the health authorities issued instructions for the eventual reopening of the pesthouse.[40]

A new Mayor, Francesco della Stufa, had recently arrived in Monte Lupo and the Health Magistracy asked him to take the position left by Father Dragoni as head of the local Health Board. Francesco della Stufa was a relatively young man – thirty-five years old[41] – and a gentleman of noble lineage. He was a fine person, but without experience, and above all, far too refined for the difficult task. In that miserable hole of Monte Lupo he had to see, hear, and cope with things that he never could have dreamed of in his Florentine palazzo – even in his worst nightmares.

His troubles began with the case of Biagio Tosi, the cobbler, whose mother had died of the plague. The young Mayor was newly in office, and his desire to show himself to be authoritative and efficient was proportionate to his basic lack of authoritativeness. When informed of the death of Tosi's mother, the Mayor ordered the cobbler and his two brothers to stay quarantined in their house. But on 16 April Tosi managed to send a complaint to the Magistracy in Florence in which he asserted that the Mayor had acted 'at the demand and instigation of certain enemies and ill-wishers', and that neither he nor his brothers had been in contact with their mother while she was sick, because they lived in separate houses. In support of his claim, Tosi included a certificate from the surgeon, Domenico Corsi, and further declared that the closing of his shop and of those of his brothers had forced 'many people' in the castello into the gutter.[42]

Probably because of the surgeon's certificate, and considering the case of little importance, the Magistracy took the complaint to be valid, and gave orders to exempt the Tosis from the quarantine. The decision was made lightly. With all the troubles and problems that the Florentine authorities had to settle, they can hardly be blamed for acting with a certain amount of carelessness in the case of a cobbler's complaint from Monte Lupo. But the decision threw Francesco della Stufa into the greatest consternation. On 12 April he hastened to write a long letter to Florence explaining the situation: in the first place, the cobbler had a sick daughter who, said the Mayor, was ill with the plague. Furthermore, it was not exactly true that the brothers Tosi and their deceased mother had not lived together when the latter was sick. It was true, that the Tosis lived in 'several houses', but those houses formed a complex and although each house had a door on the public street, on the inside they were intercommunicating; the inhabitants of each could pass from one house to another without being noticed. Taking advantage of the special structure of their buildings, the Tosis had ventured to misrepresent their separation and to claim freedom of movement. 'And I will not grant it,' protested the young aristocrat.

There are people who because of their biomass, physical dignity or psychic energy, easily assert their authority on others. Francesco della Stufa was not like that. In his report to the Magistracy in Florence he actually mentioned another regrettable incident. The mother of one, Marco Donati, a young man about twenty, had died. Having heard 'from a reliable source' that the son had taken care of his dying mother, the Mayor had ordered him to stay quarantined in his house. Taking no notice of the Mayor's order, the young Donati went 'publicly about the castello for three days', and, as though that were not enough, he managed to insult the Mayor in public: 'Having met me in the public streets he accosted me and in the presence of many said that whoever says

that he had attended his mother is a despicable cuckold.'
Hearing himself called a 'despicable cuckold' in public
nearly gave the Mayor apoplexy. He angrily called a
guard and ordered him to arrest Donati, but the guard
shrugged his shoulders and refused to touch the culprit
on the grounds that if Donati were infected, he, the guard,
had no intention of coming near and catching the disease
himself.[43] The Magistracy reacted as the Mayor had
hoped and issued orders that the Tosis be quarantined
and the young Donati arrested.[44] But the Mayor could not
make himself either obeyed or respected. 'They abuse and
despise me,' he lamented, 'and if this is not remedied by
your lordships I shall have to leave and reside outside the
castello.' Nobody listened to him. A man died of the
plague and the Mayor ordered two gravediggers to bury
the corpse immediately; the two gravediggers not only
refused to obey, but answered 'with arrogant words' that
until their salaries were paid they had no intention of
removing the dead. The gravediggers were under orders
not to mix with the population, but those two 'come out
and go through the square and everywhere else solely to
show contempt of my orders.' These querulous words were
written by the young Mayor on 1 May. The next day the
Florentine Magistracy gave him prompt support. He was
to take guards from Empoli and arrest the offenders, particularly the two shameless gravediggers. The latter were
to be given two 'twists' immediately and told to resume
their duties at once, under pain of being sent to the
galleys; and all other offenders were to receive two twists;
but those deserving greater punishment were to be pros-
ecuted and put in prison until the Health Magistracy of
Florence decided on their fate.

The authorities thought they had made themselves

clear, but a few days later they received another despairing letter from the Mayor, who wrote to the Magistracy like an unhappy little boy asking his father for aid and comfort. The affair of Marco Donati, who had called him a despicable cuckold, still rankled and the Mayor mentioned it again. But this was not the last piece of insolence he had to suffer. 'Biagio Mengheri had also wandered about the Castello all night' although he was quarantined. And those accursed gravediggers, ordered to do their duty under pain of the galleys, had replied that they would throw 'the dead in front of the Mayor's house'. The unhappy man reported in self-justification that as soon as he arrived in Monte Lupo he had caused 'a pulley to be set up in order to intimidate them', but for those Monte Lupans more was needed: 'They are not people to fear threats because they neither desire nor respect orders.'[45]

A reply came from Florence on 10 May. The authorities sought to infuse della Stufa with energy and courage, promising him extra guards, and exhorting him 'to make himself obeyed'.[46] But the young Mayor's troubles were not over. Reinforcements came from Empoli, but the guards refused to go near those suspected of the plague; the gravediggers were again told that the penalty for their conduct was the galleys, but they took no notice and 'replied most arrogantly that they would work no more'; and as if that were not enough they buried two corpses dead of the plague 'next to the residence of Cavaliere Menderi, and when sought out by me, they replied most arrogantly that they would not go to the cemetery because it was too far.'[47] The Mayor's monotonous complaints make it abundantly clear that he considered the Monte Lupans to be 'most arrogant'. The

Health Magistracy realized this and replied on 13 May, saying that it would dispatch more guards and advising the Mayor to subject the rascally gravediggers to further 'twists'.[48] The letters asking and promising help between Monte Lupo and Florence crossed one another; in the Castello the 'twists' were freely administered, but as the discouraged Mayor repeated, 'These people will not be curbed.'[49]

Amid this confusion the plague spread rapidly, encouraged both by the misery and lawlessness of the people. On 29 April the Mayor reported that in Monte Lupo 'twenty-five houses had been closed and we continually find more people sick with the contagious disease.'[50] By 1 May the number of quarantined houses had risen to thirty, and the Mayor wisely suggested 'that it would be good to reopen the pesthouse.'[51] Sixteen days later 'at the change of the moon' 25 newly-infected persons were found in the village. In view of the gravity of the situation, it was decided to delay no longer and to reopen the pesthouse 'in great haste'. But as usual, funds were lacking and the good Mayor, having none at his disposal, dipped into his own pocket in spite of being convinced 'that he could not be reimbursed until after harvest, for these people are greatly exhausted.'[52] He wrote this on 18 May. On 4 June, according to a notation in the parish book of the dead, Mayor Francesco della Stufa, 'passed to a better life', and the gravediggers who had caused him so much trouble in his life buried him after his death 'in the cemetery of Cacciacane, because he had died of the plague.'[53]

After Father Dragoni had resigned as head of the Health

Board in Monte Lupo, the Mayor had taken over that duty. As we have seen, the deputies of Public Health in the castello were an uneducated lot and unsuited to the task. They themselves knew this and openly admitted it; they needed someone to direct them, but fate seemed determined to be unkind. First, Father Dragoni sent in his resignation, and then in the very middle of the renewed epidemic they lost the Mayor. The letter which the deputies sent to Florence announcing della Stufa's death clearly shows their total bewilderment – even in the wrong date on the letter: 4 May 1631, when it was actually written on 4 June.[54] In a frenzy, the deputies informed the Health Magistracy that 'in this hour it has pleased God to call to Himself our worshipful Mayor, Commissioner of Health, by reason of which we are left dismayed and without guidance.' And they explain the reason for their dismay: 'Until now we have left the direction of each and every matter to the said worshipful Mayor without intervention on our part and we have put everything in his Worship's hands.' The Mayor had taken the initiative of admitting to the pesthouse not only the sick from the castello but also those from the whole district, to the extent that at the time of writing there were only five patients from Monte Lupo and nearly forty from the district. 'This was the Mayor's will and there was no possibility to gainsay him.' The admission of the sick from the countryside had obviously increased expenses and the worried deputies noted that 'as yet the income and outlay have not been reckoned, but we know for certain that the outlay has been much greater.' What were they to do in such a predicament? 'We have no plans,' they declared, and then they added with pathetic candour: 'We appeal to your lordships to give us a head with

35

authority. . . . By ourselves we are not sufficiently experienced to deal with such an important matter.' They closed with a wish: 'If that Father who was in charge would be willing to attend, he would be of great help to the castello.' The Father alluded to was obviously Father Dragoni.

Meanwhile the speed of events caused a series of hitches in the correspondence. The Health Magistracy had learned of the Mayor's illness, and rightly fearing that this would have an adverse effect on the Health Service they had written the following message to the Mayor's chancellor: 'We hear that the Mayor, your superior, is unwell. Therefore, you will be taking his place for all that concerns health affairs, and if you chance to be elsewhere than in Monte Lupo, return to that locality in order to carry out whatever you may be ordered to do from day to day.'[55] The letter is dated 4 June 1631. The Magistracy had no idea that as the letter was being dictated in Florence, the Mayor was breathing his last in Monte Lupo.

The Magistracy's letter arrived in Monte Lupo on 6 June. The Mayor was dead and the chancellor was not there because he had been dismissed a week earlier by the Mayor for reasons unknown to us. The letter was therefore handed over to the health deputies, who began to pass it from one to the other as if it were a hot potato. The poor men could not guess what was in the letter – it might have contained highly confidential material, and no one wanted to take the responsibility of opening it. It was a comic situation, but it certainly did not seem comic to the deputies who only decided to act when encouraged by one of the guards: 'By a verbal order from Sergeant

36

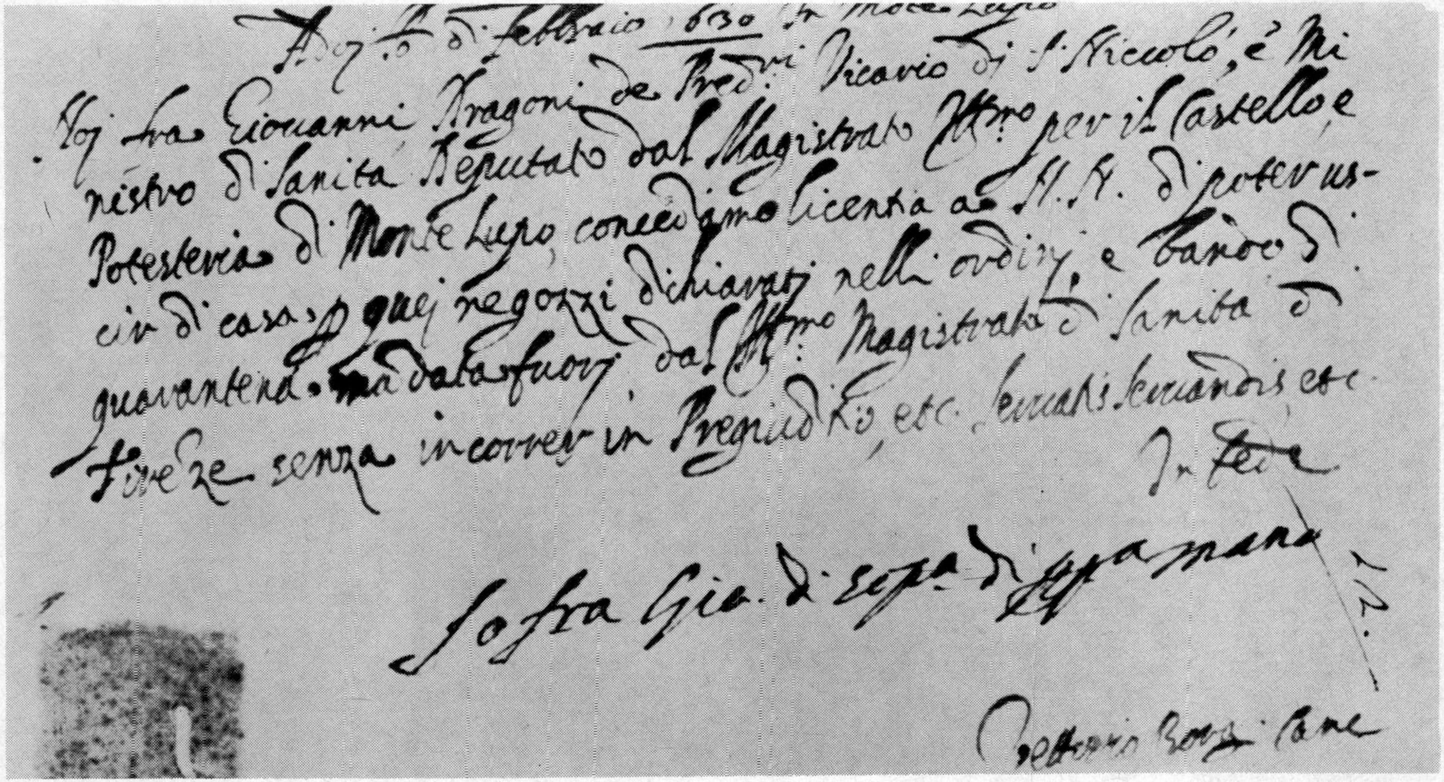

A dì 7 di Febbraio 1630 in Monte Lupo

Noi fra Giovanni Dragoni de Predi. Vicario di S. Niccolò, e Mi-
nistro di Sanità deputato dal Magistrato Ill.mo per il Castello e
Potesteria di Monte Lupo, concediamo licenza a [illegible] di poter us-
cir di casa per quei negozi dichiarati nelli ordini e bandi di
quarantena mandati fuori dal Ill.mo Magistrato di Sanità di
Firenze senza incorrer in pregiudizio, etc. servatis servandis etc.

In fede

Io fra Gio. di [illegible] di propria mano

Vettorio Borgi Canc.

Fig. 5 Being short of printed health passes (see p. 27), Father Dragoni had to issue handwritten passes. The facsimile reproduced in this figure was written by Vittorio Borgi, Chancellor to Father Dragoni and signed by the latter

1. Lazzaretto di S. Pancratio primo Lazzaretto che serui per li Brutti.

Fig. 6   The 'pulley' which was used to inflict corporal punishment on those who violated the orders of the Health Officers. In the background, this picture shows the pesthouse of St. Pancrazio in Rome during the epidemic of plague of 1656-7

Berardi we have taken the liberty of opening such a letter.' After reading it they heaved a sigh of relief – it contained nothing secret or confidential. The deputies hastened to reply to the Magistracy that the chancellor was absent, that since the Mayor had departed this life they had taken the liberty of opening the letter and, in any case, they were able to give assurance that as far as the Health Board in Monte Lupo was concerned 'no diligence was wanting.' They added optimistically that things were improving in the castello, although the epidemic was raging in the countryside.[56]

While the deputies in Monte Lupo were composing their message to Florence, the Florentine Health Magistracy was drawing up another letter addressed to Monte Lupo. It was Friday, 6 June. The news of the Mayor's death on 4 June had not yet reached Florence. The reopening of the pesthouse at Monte Lupo had been approved on 24 May,[57] but the Mayor's illness had occurred since then and the Magistracy was now concerned with finding someone capable and trustworthy to superintend the management of the hospital. The Magistrates had no doubt as to who this someone should be and they wrote to Father Dragoni asking him to serve as 'Superintendent of that pesthouse in the same manner as you were in the months past.'[58] Without realizing it, the Magistrates were fulfilling the wish expressed by the health deputies of Monte Lupo in their letter of 4 June, which had not yet been delivered.

On 9 June, in view of the grave situation in that area, the Health Magistracy in Florence again decreed the isolation of Monte Lupo. Stockades were re-erected at the gates of the castello and the inhabitants were notified 'that they should not dare to leave their community on pain of death, or of being killed with impunity, as outlaws, by any person finding them outside their community either with or without a health pass.'[59] Monte Lupo was back where it was months before.

Of course Father Dragoni 'obeyed'. He took over the management of the pesthouse, and subsequently the duties of head of the Health Board as well. But the situation was very difficult, even for a man of his ability. The Magistracy had decided to concentrate all the sick from the surrounding district in the pesthouse at Monte Lupo, but, because of the extent of the epidemic, that pesthouse was no longer adequate. Around 20 June, the Health Magistracy in Florence sent the surgeon, Coveri to superintend the opening of a second pesthouse,[60] but the sick flocked there in such crowds that even the second lazaretto was not enough. On the 28th, Father Dragoni wrote despairingly to Florence: 'The sick from the district have multiplied at such a rate that the two pesthouses are insufficient to receive them.' 'If I have to let the sick people here die in their own homes,' lamented the Father, 'the whole of Monte Lupo will be but a pesthouse.' The influx of so many infected persons from outside had also aroused strong feelings among the Monte Lupans. 'The few who are left here, rebellious and frightened, say that they want to retreat to the country, and I am obliged to defend my own life and health in my own household.' What was the Father alluding to in this last remark? To tensions arising in his own convent and an increasing hostility towards himself? It is not clear, but what is clear is that the Father considered the situation intolerable:

'I do not believe that your lordships desire the impossible from me.'[61]

Burglaries also began again. *Il Macchia,* who had already been caught in January for robbery, was back at work, this time with the help of his sister-in-law.[62] But worse crimes occurred on 20 July and the days following. Our information about these misdeeds is documented by the reports of the guards and by a series of interrogations held in the instructional phase of the prosecution. The first interrogation took place on 22 July in the presence of Father Dragoni.[63] The others were held before Health Commissioner Benedetto Sacchetti between 23 July and 9 August.[64] Besides these documents, and complementing them, there are also extracts from the 'book of copies and records belonging to the Health Board at Monte Lupo' kept by Father Dragoni's registrar, Vittorio Borgi,[65] as well as various correspondence, results of inquiries, and miscellaneous records.[66] These sources provide us with a clear picture of the events.

IV

IN THE parish church of Monte Lupo there was – and is – a horrifying crucifix (see Fig. 7). The cross itself is wretched, and the Christ is contorted in agony and covered with bleeding wounds. A purely rational observer might wonder how and why a community already full of tortured, suffering, and wounded people could want to look on such a dreadful image. But people are not wholly rational. Perhaps the parishioners of Monte Lupo found pleasure in thinking that the Son of God had suffered pains like theirs, and would therefore be willing to persuade his Almighty Father to suspend the punishment that He had gone to such lengths to inflict upon the sinful people of Tuscany. However, such subtleties are beyond the scope of this present essay, and all that needs to be said is that there was such a crucifix in Monte Lupo, that people believed in its miraculous properties, and that this same crucifix was carried in procession through the village on suitable occasions. So what more fitting occasion than the onslaught of the plague to bring the miraculous crucifix out of the church and stage a procession? The priest of Monte Lupo, Don Antonio Bontadi, had no doubts at all.

At that time, the Commissioner-General for Public Health for that portion of the valley of the Arno River was the nobleman Benedetto Sacchetti, who had succeeded Commissioner Gondi. Benedetto Sacchetti belonged

41

to one of the most illustrious patrician families of Florence; he was a Knight of the Order of Jerusalem, and as such had fought against the Turks in the galleys of his Order. In 1631 Benedetto Sacchetti was 48 years old,[1] an energetic man of action, accustomed to command, and one may be sure that, having fought against the Turks, he would not be the type to let himself be pushed around or called a 'despicable cuckold' like poor Mayor della Stufa.

In his capacity as Commissioner-General of Public Health, Cavalier Sacchetti travelled from one village to another in his district with his retinue of registrar-clerk, corporal, and several guards, making inspections, issuing ordinances, deciding such penalties as came within his jurisdictional and executive powers, and sending reports to the Health Magistracy in Florence. Shortly after the middle of July, Benedetto Sacchetti was in San Gimignano, and there, like a bolt from the blue, came the news that on Sunday, 20 July (to use Sacchetti's words), 'Antonio Bontardi, parish priest of Monte Lupo, intended to have a procession displaying a crucifix held in great devotion there, and inviting all the neighbouring communities.' Benedetto Sacchetti respected religion and was a member of a religious order himself, but like all men in the service of the Magistracy of Public Health, he did not look favourably on processions and popular assemblies in times of plague. Besides, Monte Lupo had been quarantined by the Florentine authorities, and by inviting the neighbouring communities to take part in the procession, the priest of Monte Lupo openly violated the orders of the Magistracy. This was a serious matter. Even more serious, the notification arrived at the eleventh hour when, by the Commissioner's own admission, 'he could no longer prevent the whole affair.'[2] At best he could try to limit the gathering of people. With this in mind and with relevant instructions, the Commissioner urgently dispatched to Monte Lupo the surgeon, Coveri.

Michelagniolo di Orazio Coveri had entered the health service at the beginning of July, when the epidemic had not yet reached Tuscany, but terrifying news was pouring in from Milan, Venice, Verona, Mantua, Parma, and – even more frightening – from nearby Bologna. In the course of July, Coveri saw and visited a great number of 'dead and sick',[3] and in August, when the Magistracy learned of suspicious cases of illness in the village of Tavola, Coveri was entrusted with the duty of visiting the sick and finding out whether they had the plague.[4] From then on the surgeon was always in the forefront of the battle against the epidemic, moving from one village to another, from one pesthouse to another, bringing orders and subsidies, and carrying out inspections and controls. He was extremely conscientious and precise, much given to the quantitative analysis of facts. His numerous reports to the Health Office in Florence are generally rich in figures and data, reflecting his methodical and punctilious nature. A typical report of his from Monte Lupo on Monday, 23 June 1631 specified that 'since 19 hours last Saturday until now, Monday, at 17 hours, 8 persons have died in the pesthouse and 4 in the Castello, which makes a total of 12.'[5] Reporting on the number of fatal cases, Coveri was not satisfied with defining the period covered in days; if possible, he would also specify the hours. Such a punctilious character was obviously a valuable asset to the Health Magistracy, but Coveri was not an easy man. He was hard, disputatious, and typically *'toscanaccio'* in

43

his rough aggressiveness. When he was sent to Prato in November 1630 to help the health authorities there to set up a pesthouse, he succeeded in alienating everyone in the place.[6] When he inspected the pesthouse at Monticello at the beginning of May 1633, one of the monks serving there reported resentfully to the Health Magistracy in Florence that 'the surgeon, Coveri appeared, and has dealt with Prior Bartolomeo and with me with much arrogance and harsh words.' And the monk went on to say:

Your Lordships, I do not believe that it can be on your orders that this man treats us with so little respect. We are here to act charitably towards these poor people for the love of God and with no other interest than in Paradise, and it seems strange to us that a surgeon had to come here and, while many were present, had to behave as a superior towards us with no respect, without knowing what he was saying, and in fact saying things that have turned the whole town upside down. . . . He told us that he has grown white hairs in the plague and has straightened up other monks; [he has used] words that he should not have used with us, as we are monks and not soldiers. May God forgive him.[7]

During October and subsequent months of 1630, Coveri made frequent visits of inspection to Monte Lupo, bearing subsidies and orders from Florence. He and Father Dragoni seem to have understood each other immediately; they were both rough characters, and they both believed in order and discipline. In Monte Lupo, however, the surgeon's inflexibility must have made him little liked, and while the people in Prato limited themselves to conspiring to nullify his proposals, those in Monte Lupo organized 'persecutions' against him, and hostility reached such a point that Coveri was afraid to go about the castello without an arquebus.[8]

The health authorities in Florence had a high opinion

of Coveri; when they sent him to Prato to arrange for the hospital, they introduced him to the local officials as an 'intelligent' person.[9] His career seemed assured when something plunged him into trouble: at the end of January 1631, Coveri was in prison. Was it for debts? For taxes? Part of the 'persecutions' by the Monte Lupans? We shall probably never know. The health authorities – undoubtedly for his protection – had him locked in their own jail, but the Public Prosecutor ordered him to be transferred to the town's prison,[10] which would indicate that his transgression had nothing to do with health affairs, or with activities carried out on behalf of the Health Board.[11] The surgeon was in prison for about a month; then he was sent into exile at Leghorn, where he remained until about the end of May.[12] However, the Health Magistracy continued to remember him with esteem and consideration. When he left prison for exile, they gave him a 'reward' of 50 *scudi*,[13] and at the end of May, after two months of exile in Leghorn, he was readmitted to the service. One might suppose that surgeons were in great demand, and that anyone would be accepted without much questioning, but at the end of the following November, when the plague was over and two of the five surgeons of the Health Board were dismissed, Coveri was one of the three retained by the Magistracy. And a year later, when the number of surgeons in the service of the Health Magistracy was finally reduced to two, Coveri was still among those who kept their jobs.[14] In January 1631, when some of the equipment of the Magistracy's local office was sold off, some boards of good timber were given to Coveri in recognition 'of his good service'.[15]

Coveri arrived in Monte Lupo in great haste on the Sunday morning of 20 July. While he rode at an early hour towards the castello, he must have been thinking about those Monte Lupans; exactly two months had elapsed since he had written to the Health Magistracy from his exile in Leghorn 'about the persecutions ordered and carried out against me by some people in Monte Lupo', and had requested 'the permit for arquebuses', because he was 'still mistrustful, fearing to be attacked while passing through that locality.'[16] To his haughty and disputatious nature, the new assignment must have appeared as a kind of nemesis; now it was up to him, Master Michelagniolo Coveri, to go to the castello to restore order and teach those Monte Lupans a lesson. But although Coveri was unaware of it, the significance of his mission went far beyond the purely personal aspects. On that July Sunday, the surgeon from the Health Magistracy represented the State, determined to assert its authority in face of the insubordinate initiative taken by men of the Church. And at the same time, not many miles from where Galileo lived, the surgeon was coming to uphold the dictates of reason against religious emotion, the teaching of 'experience' against the assumptions of faith. Paradoxically, the first person whom the humble knight of reason and the State had to meet and agree with on a course of action was indeed the legitimate local representative of the State – but also a man of the Church and a monk, Father Giovanni Dragoni. Those who like to interpret history only in terms of abstract classes and categories might expect to read of a violent confrontation between the monk and the surgeon. But history is made by men and not by categories. Father Dragoni and Coveri knew each other from the preceding autumn, and the two

46

men respected one another. Moreover, Father Dragoni, in spite of being a monk, did not approve of the defiant initiative taken by the priest of the Castello.

When Coveri arrived in Monte Lupo on Sunday morning, he found 'that the procession was getting ready to start, and there was a huge concourse of people.' The surgeon knew the district and its people very well, and he was not the man to miss significant details; he noticed immediately that among those gathered for the procession were 'five from Pontorme, where mortality from the plague is higher.'[17] In fact, Pontorme, in which there were 340 souls before the plague, had had 41 deaths, and at the moment when Coveri made his observation, another 25 were patients in the pesthouse.[18] What was to be done in these circumstances? As Commissioner Sacchetti had foreseen, it was too late to forbid the procession. The only thing possible was to try to reduce as far as they could the number of Monte Lupans assembling – especially as the inhabitants of neighbouring villages had begun to stream in, taking no notice of ordinances, guards, or barriers. The Father and the surgeon came to rapid agreement: following Sacchetti's instructions, it was proclaimed in furious haste 'that women and children should not leave their homes.' Conscientious to the point of pedantry, both the Father and the surgeon thought that the proclamation was possibly not enough, that people would use the excuse of not having been warned in time; so they ordered three guards to go immediately 'from house to house, telling women and children not to go out.' All this was in vain. It was like preaching to the wind: the church was soon packed with men and women, boys and girls, who had come to gaze at and adore the crucifix.

The religious ceremonies of pre-industrial days were

47

not hasty affairs. So the 'happening' of Sunday morning was only the first phase of a complex series of events. On the same day, the psalms and the procession were to be repeated in the evening. Chastened by the morning's failure, Coveri sent two guards with Corporal Agostino Chiatti to the parish church 'to prevent women and children from going to Vespers so as not to make a large gathering.' Standing there was Don Antonio Bontadi, priest of the Church of St. Giovanni Evangelista – still a young man, 28 years old,[19] with a sanguine and quarrelsome nature. Don Antonio immediately began to wrangle with the guards, telling them 'to go away and mind their own business.' The guards pretended neither to see nor hear. Their job was to try 'to prevent women and children who refused to obey the proclamation against entering the church.' If it was impossible to keep them at home, at least they should not crowd into the church. But the priest went on and on, getting more and more heated, and at a certain point, when he saw the guards were not leaving, 'he came up to me,' testified Corporal Chiatti, 'and asked me what I wanted. I replied that I had been sent by the health officers to disperse the crowd of women and children. Then the aforementioned reverend replied that we should go away and let everyone pass because he wanted to have all his people with him and did not wish to send anyone away, and if we did not leave, they would persuade us with arquebus shots.'

It was difficult for Corporal Chiatti to argue with the priest. A priest was an authority in the village, and more important still, a priest could not be roughed up or arrested; between the guards and Don Bontadi lay the delicate relationship between Church and State, and to proceed against an ecclesiastic required a special permit from His Serene Highness the Grand Duke. In the specific case of Monte Lupo, there was yet another compelling factor. At the priest's side was a threatening populace ready to lend strong hands against the guards. Worse still, at the entrance to the church were two gun-racks with several arquebuses, placed there because at the end of every procession it was customary to fire salutes in honour of the crucifix. With those arquebuses nearby and the menacing faces of the crowd pressing around the priest, Don Antonio's threats sounded anything but rhetorical. The corporal and the two guards beat a hasty retreat, ran to Coveri, who was with Father Dragoni, and told him how they had been 'threatened'.

Coveri was not a man to let this pass. He took the guards and returned furiously to the church. Don Antonio was still there, more excited than ever, now surrounded by other priests and by many other people, among whom was an obstreperous fellow named Antonio di Pavolo Giunti of Monte Lupo, a baker by trade, who was always to the fore when it came to organizing festivals.[20] As soon as Don Antonio saw Coveri and the guards, he 'came forward with Antonio the baker and said: "What do you want here? If you don't leave, I shall make you go with arquebus shots." ' Coveri's only reply was to order the guards to remove the arquebuses from the gun-racks and to take them to Father Dragoni at the health offices. The baker then advanced and began to 'argue loudly' with Coveri. At the court of inquiry which followed the incident, the investigators wished to know 'whether the said baker, Antonio, was armed and what kind of arms he had.' Corporal Chiatti reported that 'he saw his dagger.' Coveri testified 'that Antonio was armed with a coat of mail and gauntlets.' Offensive words flew between Coveri

49

and the baker. At the inquiry, the investigators pressed for details of this exchange, but the corporal got out of it by saying that the baker 'was in support of the priest, but he [the corporal] was not listening.' And Coveri, when asked what words were spoken, replied, 'I don't remember because I was angry, but they were contemptuous.'

Coveri succeeded in having the arquebuses removed, but otherwise there was little he could do. As the guard, Michele da Piacenza testified at the inquiry: 'Because there were so few of us, we could not keep the women from entering [the church].' Coveri and the guards retreated in good order: 'It was advisable for us to leave,' admitted the corporal. Don Antonio was exultant. 'The same evening there was another procession in which all the women and children joined. . . . All the women and children of Monte Lupo were there.' Then, following the tradition of pre-industrial festivals, 'many people feasted in the Church', and 'many persons ate and drank together after the procession.'

By now the situation was completely out of control. The next day, Monday, 21 July, the Registrar of Public Health noted in his 'book of copies and records': 'I record that on this morning the people of Fibbiana came in procession: women, men, children, for about an hour. . . . The same day there were people of all sorts of conditions and from various places, as many men as women.' Coveri, in great alarm, had sent men to the gates, but, faced with swarms of psalm-singing men, women, and children, the few guards could do little or nothing. The barriers at the gates were open, and the guards 'could not turn back anyone, even though they came from Empoli, Pontorme, and Cortenuova.' It was an unending Babel. On the evening of the 21st, a procession was formed for the nth time

– on this occasion made up of 'two contingents from Monte Lupo, men, women and boys, girls and small children, and all with many strangers in a great crowd, and it went on until about two hours after sunset.' As usual the psalms finished gloriously, that is, with feasting and drinking.

The night was warm. Everyone was in that state of excitement that was usual at country festivals. About two hours after sunset, the women and children went home, but some of the men remained in the castello's alleys to work off the alcohol and the excitement. In violation of the quarantine to which all people serving in the pesthouse were subject, Bernardino Zampetti, surgeon, and Jacopo Casini, apothecary, both in service at the pesthouse, had arranged with three lute players in the castello to go and 'serenade a young girl' in San Miniatello, a village within an arquebus shot of Monte Lupo. The group had met and were proceeding towards the gate that opened on to the road to San Miniatello when they fell in with another festive but larger band who had no intention of going home and who could have hoped for nothing more to their taste. Nobody gave a second thought to the plague, the crucifix, or the processions; shouting and singing, one group following the other at a distance of about thirty yards, the small crowd moved towards the walls of the castello. At the gate there was the stockade that had been closed at nightfall after the visitors from outside the village had left. After all the coming and going during the day and evening to adore the crucifix, the precaution of closing the stockade at night might be thought ridiculous. But the directives of the Health Magistracy were peremptory, and, if it had been impossible to keep out dozens of psalm-singers during the day when the stockade was open, the guards could offer their own inadequate numbers as excuse; but, if they left the stockade open at night, they could not disclaim responsibility. In any case, the stockade that had been useless to keep out neighbouring villagers during the day was of no effect in keeping the merry party of the night of the 21st inside the castello. As the surgeon himself was to testify at the court of inquiry: 'We went out of the gate at Monte Lupo in the direction of San Miniatello through a gap in the stockade where a plank was missing.' A monk also joined the group – Father Agostino da Firenze – and a young cleric who was the servant of the monk, but they, according to the records of the inquiry, were not going 'to serenade the young girl', but 'to hear confessions at the pesthouse on the road to San Miniatello.'

'Near the gate leading to San Miniatello' lived Pandolfo di Tommaso Giorgi of Monte Lupo. He must have been inquisitive by nature, but the fact that his windows over-looked the main gate of the castello must in the course of time have further developed his innate curiosity. On the evening of 21 July, Pandolfo was awakened by the shouts of the company going to San Miniatello. Anyone else would have uttered a few curses, turned over in bed, and minded his own business. But not Pandolfo; he ran to the window full of curiosity about other people's business and, by the light of the torches that some of the party were carrying, recognized the surgeon and the apothecary from the penthouse, Tommaso Brizelli, the lute player, Biagio Tosi, the cobbler who had insulted Mayor della Stufa, and some others.

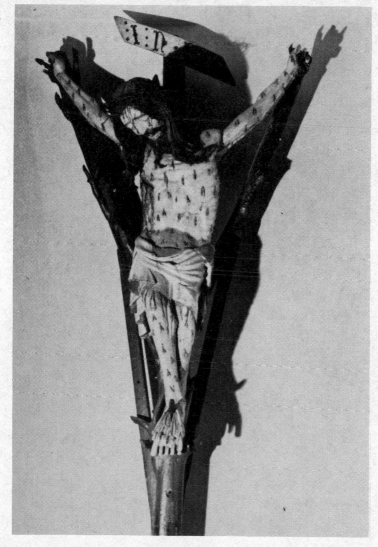

Fig. 7 The miraculous crucifix of Monte Lupo

Fig. 8　A section of the walls of Monte Lupo with one of the gates

One by one the merrymakers squeezed through the gap in the stockade and disappeared outside the wall. Silence and darkness returned to the streets, and Pandolfo went back to bed. But he was fated not to sleep that night. Shortly afterwards, he again heard unusual sounds – though not human voices this time. He heard 'a board fall and a nail scrape.' So he ran to the window again. He made a noise opening it, and, as his courage was in inverse proportion to his curiosity, 'every few minutes he had to draw back inside, because he was afraid of being hit by stones.' Nevertheless, he managed to distinguish in the darkness 'three or four men who were not speaking but working away in silence, and all were armed.' It was plain that 'they were removing' the stockade.

Then the noises stopped and the shadowy figures disappeared. But from then on it was impossible for Pandolfo to sleep. Time passed – how much, he had no idea. Then the serenaders who had gone to San Miniatello returned. At the gate they received a shock. The stockade was no longer there: it had been removed, or destroyed, or had simply vanished. The surgeon was the first to realize the gravity of the situation. Destruction of the stockade was obviously an act of open defiance; it was an explicit insult to the powerful authority of the Magistracy of Public Health. Appalled, the surgeon began to yell. Pandolfo, who was keeping out of sight behind his window, but in a state of intense excitement, could not restrain himself. He came out of hiding and shouted to the surgeon not to be alarmed: he, Pandolfo, had seen it all and could testify that the surgeon had had nothing to do with the destruction of the stockade.

Neither Pandolfo nor the surgeon nor any other members of the party suspected that another offence against the Health Department had been committed that night in Monte Lupo. *Il Macchia*, who was a mattress-maker by day and a thief by night, had been arrested the day before on suspicion of robbing a house contaminated by the plague. Considered as possibly infected, he was not put in jail, but in compliance with the health regulations was confined to his own house, which was nailed up with bars on the outside. Now, on that same night, the bars on *Il Macchia's* house had also been removed.

Coveri had left Monte Lupo on the afternoon or evening of the 21st in haste to warn the Commissioner of the turn events were taking in the castello. The storm therefore broke on the shoulders of Father Dragoni. He was awakened hastily at dawn on the 22nd and given various versions of the misdeeds of the night. Some alarmed villagers had realized that the situation was completely out of hand and feared reprisals from the Magistracy of Health. Those who might be suspected rushed to the Father to present their alibis, and, as often happens in such cases, those anxious to divert suspicion from themselves encouraged rumours that would throw it on others. Vittorio Borgi, Father Dragoni's official Registrar for the Health Board, made the following entry in his journal:

July 22, 1631. Last night the bars were removed from *Il Macchia's* house, quarantined the day before because of suspected theft from an infected house, and the stockade at the main gate of the Castello was also removed. The bars were found in the square, and the timbers of the stockade remained hidden until the twentieth hour that day behind the wall of the Castello, and some of them were found in a hut belonging to the nuns of *Il Paradiso*.

Depositions. Early in the morning Biagio Tosi appeared and said that at three after sunset he went to a party at San Miniatello, and the stockade was there then, but when he returned it had been removed and taken away. Antonio Forzini and Vincenzo Bardi stated the same thing. The surgeon came to excuse himself after being accused in front of Father Giovanni Dragoni of removing the stockade from the gate, which he asserted was not true, and in support of this he requested that they summoned Pandolfo Giorgio, living nearby, who had said that he had heard and seen that it was not the surgeon.

To add to the confusion, on that same morning of Tuesday the 22nd, all the inhabitants of the nearby village of Capraia, men, women, boys, and girls, arrived at the castello in procession, singing and chanting psalms, to see and worship the crucifix.

It is doubtful if Father Dragoni would have called on the crucifix for help. Whether he invoked any saint at all is known only to God. What is certain is that he made an urgent appeal to Commissioner Sacchetti. In great haste he wrote a letter, telegraphic in style, entrusting the messenger with confidential communications to be reported orally: 'There followed many disorders and transgressions on the same day that the display and procession of the Holy Crucifix took place,' reported the Father. 'They made small formations with arms to prevent the health authority from operating. And that night the bars on one house and the stockade at the gate were removed and all the wood carried away. Thefts were discovered.' The Father praised the surgeon's work: 'Signor Coveri issued sound orders. He removed the arms and had them deposited in my care.' Father Dragoni's shafts were directed at another target: 'It is necessary to take measures against these agitators of the people. I cannot put everything on paper. I have sent a messenger for this reason. The evidence is serious, and to tell you in confidence and under seal of secrecy, the reverend parish priest is largely responsible for these uprisings. By word of mouth I shall report all the details, so that you can take appropriate measures. Your presence is needed.'[21]

It is really unfortunate that the delicate nature of the subject prevented Father Dragoni from putting 'everything on paper', and that he had to entrust the more explosive details to the messenger for oral delivery. The accusation with respect to the priest was extremely serious, although Father Dragoni was not the only one in the village to consider it true. Agostino Chiatti, the corporal of the guards, reporting at the court of inquiry about the affair of the stockade, stated that 'people say that the priest had had it removed, as he went around saying that in times when the Crucifix was brought out, the gates should remain open.'

Father Dragoni's feelings in this awkward situation are not difficult to imagine. 'Your presence is needed,' he wrote to the Commissioner, and added, 'I have also written to Signor Coveri, asking him to come with guards, at the same time if possible.' The sexagenarian monk was obviously feeling isolated. The sense of loneliness was probably heightened by the fact that in this critical moment his own logical mind had placed him, a man of the Church and the Faith, in the opposite camp of reason and the State.

Meanwhile, he was not idle. The stockade had been broken down, and the honour and prestige of the Health Magistracy required the identification and exemplary punishment of the authors of the crime. Many different rumours were circulating in the village. Some accused the priest of having incited his adherents to pull down the stockade; others put forward the name of Bernardino Zampetti, the surgeon who had gone to serenade the girl at San Miniatello, but who, as we have seen, had hurried to Father Dragoni on the morning of Tuesday the 22nd to establish his innocence and to bring Pandolfo's evidence into play. Furthermore, Pandolfo himself had not calmed down, but as soon as it was light had gone through the village where the affair of the stockade was being hotly discussed and had begun excitedly telling everyone that he had seen it all and that he, Pandolfo, knew just what had happened. Later, when evidence was being heard, Corporal Chiatti was asked if he knew 'by whom the said stockade had been removed' and he replied, 'I do not know. There is a man called Pandolfo who lives by the gate that leads to San Miniatello; he heard the noise and recognized two people. He will tell you.' The corporal was evidently reporting the opinion held generally in the village, which Pandolfo himself had encouraged by his eager chattering.

Like so many talkative people who can hardly believe that they have been for an instant at the centre of exceptional events, Pandolfo must have felt pleasantly self-important and authoritative on that Tuesday morning as he went around boasting that he knew exactly what had gone on the night before. But his moment of glory and exhilaration was destined to be short-lived.

Rumours spread quickly in small communities like Monte Lupo, and the people who had reason to fear they would be accused or even merely suspected soon visited Pandolfo and gave him to understand by threatening looks and words that he had better keep his mouth shut. Pandolfo, who had been inordinately puffed up at being at the centre of things, suddenly found himself deflated and began to wish he had never gone to the window to satisfy his curiosity about the nocturnal events. His chagrin reached a climax when the guards came and ordered him to go with them. Father Dragoni wanted to identify the authors of the crime and, according to the local rumour, Pandolfo was in a position to tell who had broken down the stockade. It was still Tuesday, 22 July, and to Pandolfo it must have seemed the longest day of his life. He had not slept at all during the night, and now in less than twenty-four hours he had experienced the whole gamut of emotions, ranging from excited curiosity to the heights of euphoria and down to the depths of terror. The guards escorted him to the Public Health office, and there Pandolfo found himself face to face with the formidable monk and his registrar.

Father Dragoni characteristically went straight to the heart of the matter. His first question was 'whether last night he had heard noises and sounds of breaking down the stockade at the gate near him.' Pandolfo cleverly tried to deflect the conversation from the incident of the stockade – obviously the most burning issue – and to direct it towards the serenaders. He replied that 'he had got up earlier because of hearing the disorderly sounds of people going to the party at San Miniatello.' Father Dragoni momentarily let himself be led in Pandolfo's chosen direction and asked 'whether he had recognized any of those people going to the party.' Pandolfo had no difficulty in answering: 'Yes; that is to say he had recognized some of them, Tommaso Brizelli who was playing the lute, Giovan Battista Lepori, Biagio Tosi, and the surgeon and

58

the apothecary from the pesthouse.' At this point, Father Dragoni, who had heard a rumour that the father confessor of the hospital had also been seen amongst the merrymakers, maliciously inquired 'whether the Father in charge of the sick was there.' Pandolfo prudently retreated: 'I did not recognize him. If he was there, he could not have been wearing his habit.' Father Dragoni did not insist, but returned to the point that Pandolfo feared: 'Had he recognized any of those who had broken down the stockade of the castello?' Pandolfo replied that 'he had not recognized them, and that every few minutes he had to withdraw inside the window because he was afraid of being stoned, as he had made a noise in opening the window. Nevertheless, he had heard a plank fall to the ground, and a large nail made a loud noise while being extracted.' By lingering on these details, Pandolfo, who was not stupid, hoped to divert attention from the central question, but Father Dragoni was not disposed to give way. Pandolfo was 'questioned again as to whether he had recognized them, as it had been reported that he had already shown himself quick to say that he had, and that he had seen that they were Biagio Tosi and Bernardino, the surgeon of the sick.' The question was insidious: it hinged on Pandolfo's loquacity in which he had indulged that morning, but the people referred to were almost certainly not the guilty ones. Pandolfo felt the circle closing in, but he did not lose heart. He replied that 'he could not say that he recognized them, only that he had seen that there were three or four of them and that they were not speaking, but working in silence, and all were armed.' This time Father Dragoni neither insisted nor pursued the hint in Pandolfo's admission of having seen that 'all were armed.' He asked some general questions about the

59

time the various actions occurred and about the serenaders. Pandolfo was probably beginning to breathe again
when Father Dragoni put a question that pulled him up
short: 'Had he spoken to anyone about this event?' How
could that devilish monk know so much? Taken by sur-
prise, Pandolfo replied shortly and simply, 'No.' Father
Dragoni, unperturbed, repeated the question. Pandolfo,
now on tenterhooks and staking his all, repeated his
answer. This went on for four rounds, until the Father
challenged the defendant, saying 'that it was positively
known that Giuliano di Andrea Mazzuoli had spoken to
him and said, 'Pandolfo, I hear that you are going around
saying that I broke down the stockade at the gate, which
you cannot say even though you were at the window.'
Pandolfo was silent. He was at a point when he no longer
knew which saint to invoke, nor even which way to turn,
when the Father told him to go home and to stay there,
locked in, to be at the disposition of the investigating
authorities. In order to avoid further intimidation, he was
'ordered not to show himself at his windows or doors,
under pain of being sent to serve in the galleys.' The command was superfluous – the last thing that Pandolfo
wanted was to look out of his window again.

The following day, Wednesday, 23 July, Commissioner
Sacchetti arrived in Monte Lupo in haste. He was furious.
He was furious with the priests who were responsible for
stirring up all this disorder; he was furious with the inhabitants of Monte Lupo who had never given him anything
but trouble, and, as for those scoundrels who had had
the nerve to break down the stockade, . . . !

The Commissioner wasted no time. He first interviewed the three guards, Corporal Antonio Chiatti, Lorenzo Scrittilli, and Michele da Piacenza, who, with the corporal as spokesman, gave him a detailed account of all that had happened, especially on Sunday the 20th, concerning the procession, the behaviour and threats of the priest, and the dispute between Coveri on one side and the priest and Antonio di Pavolo Giunti on the other. After hearing these statements, which confirmed in detail what he had already learned from Coveri and Father Dragoni, the Commissioner unhesitatingly decided to initiate a formal court of inquiry, thus setting in motion a legal action. The substance of what had occurred was summarized for the official record, and interrogations began in the presence of the Commissioner and his registrar. The first person to be questioned was Antonio Chiatti, the corporal of the guards, who repeated what he had said in his earlier report. Next was the guard, Michele da Piacenza, who confirmed the corporal's statement. At this point, the Commissioner, still angry, sent for Pandolfo. The poor wretch was staying shut up in his house, keeping far away from all windows as he had promised. Probably he would have been willing to stay there forever if required, but along came the guards, and in less than twenty-four hours after the earlier questioning, Pandolfo was brought before Benedetto Sacchetti, Commissioner-General of the Magistracy of Health, a nobleman of Florence, a Knight of the Order of Malta, and furious into the bargain.

The first question was short and sharp, and the tone augured no good: 'Where do you live in Monte Lupo?' 'I live near the gate that leads to San Miniatello,' replied Pandolfo, doubtless wishing that God had willed his house be situated in any other part of the castello. The Commissioner then asked 'whether that evening, in spite of being indoors, he had heard any noise.' Pandolfo answered coherently with a statement similar to the one he had given the day before: 'I heard a noise – that is, I heard a plank fall and a nail screech. I went to the window and saw three people at the gate, breaking it down.' The Commissioner promptly asked: 'Who were they who were breaking down the stockade?' Pandolfo replied equally promptly: 'I did not recognize them because it was dark.' The Commissioner then put an insidious question: 'What were they breaking it with?' If Pandolfo had been able to distinguish the tools used to break up the barrier, then he was lying when he asserted that he could not distinguish the evildoers. The trap did not work. Pandolfo replied: 'I could not see, because I drew back inside, being afraid they might see me and throw stones at me, and one of them had a sword.' The Commissioner was insistent: 'Were they young or old?' Pandolfo was equally firm: 'I could not recognize them.' But the Commissioner did not give up: 'How were they dressed?' Pandolfo stood his ground for the nth time, saying coherently: 'I do not know because I could not recognize them as it was dark.'

Realizing that he could not extract any useful information, the Commissioner made a diversion with two questions about the serenaders, but then returned to the main point and asked 'whether he had heard anyone say who had removed the stockade.' Pandolfo, mindful of what Father Dragoni had confronted him with the day before, answered: 'I have not heard it mentioned. Master Giuliano di Antonio Mazzuoli came to see me and yelled at me that he had heard that I had said it was he who had done the breaking down.'

At this juncture, the Commissioner, who had exhausted his stock of patience, resorted to threats: 'He must make up his mind to tell who it was that he had seen breaking down the stockade; otherwise, he would be locked up for a while.' Pandolfo did not let himself be intimidated and consistently replied: 'I cannot tell who they were because I did not recognize them.' Unfortunately for him, the Commissioner was not a man to make idle threats. He turned to the guards and abruptly ordered them to put Pandolfo in jail.

We have no documents describing the jail at Monte Lupo, but it was doubtless an unpleasant hole, and we shall never know whether Pandolfo managed to sleep that night or not. It is not unlikely that he spent a long time in the darkness lamenting the fact that in all the village, and after all that had happened, the only person to land in jail was himself, Pandolfo, who had stayed quietly at home on the night of the crimes – and all because he had had the unlucky idea of getting out of bed to peer out of the window.

Coveri was due to come back to Monte Lupo, and perhaps it was in anticipation of his arrival that no further interrogations were held on the 24th. The surgeon was in the village on Friday, 25 July, and was immediately summoned by the Commissioner, who asked him to recount in detail 'what went on in Monte Lupo during the day of the 20th of this month.' Coveri made his deposition and spoke in detail of those who 'did not respect the edict', of the priest, Antonio Bontadi and of his insolent and rebellious behaviour; he reported on Antonio the baker, more obstreperous and insolent than the priest, and hinted that the same Antonio and some of his adherents could have been involved in the matter of the stockade: 'That Antonio and three or four others, companions of his, are insolent because they smash stockades and make a great thing of it from what I hear.'

The judicial taking of evidence was not complete, but the Commissioner now had enough material in hand to send a report to the Health Magistracy in Florence, and he hastened to write and send it the same day, 25 July.[22] He reported that 'while I was in San Gimignano, Antonio Bontadi, parish priest of Monte Lupo, wished to conduct a procession, displaying a crucifix held there in greatest reverence, and he had invited all the people from the neighbouring district, and, having learned of this by chance and being unable to be there, I sent Coveri.' He added that Coveri had acted commendably, but that 'the numerous and not very obedient people had little respect for Coveri and the edict.' He described in detail how Coveri and the guards were confronted by the priest, Bontadi 'with a following of others of the Castello'. All that commotion, according to the Commissioner, had had unfortunate consequences on the course of the epidemic: 'As a result, the disease, which seemed checked, [re-appeared] after that day, [and] among the people who had come to the ceremony we found [that] several [became] sick, who were [then] taken to the pesthouse, most of them women.' Clearly the Commissioner knew how to strike the right note to make the Health Magistrates prick up their ears and encourage them to approve energetic measures against the troublemakers of Monte Lupo. The Commissioner reiterated the argument at the end of his report, stating that: 'Until last Sunday the disease had somewhat abated; although it does not seem to have made much progress in Monte Lupo and outside, nevertheless, since Sunday nine people have gone to the pesthouse.' Behind this insistence there was a firm conviction to which we shall return presently. At any rate, the Commissioner was also determined not to let the wrongdoers off lightly. 'I am proceeding against the priest and the others. I have confined the priest to his house under pain of 300 *scudi* payable to the State Treasury; as to the others, they will get their due.' There is no grain of indulgence in these words; their author was obviously still boiling with anger, and the outburst, 'the others will get their due,' did not augur well for the ringleaders of Monte Lupo. Commissioner Sacchetti was made of different stuff from Mayor della Stufa.

In his report the Commissioner also mentioned that he had written to the Vicar of the Archbishopric in Florence 'to let him know that there are other priests in the neighbouring villages who after this example are planning to display some of their sacred images, which, for my part, I do not approve.' The Commissioner had asked the Vicar 'to be good enough to forbid the priests to conduct [the processions]'. Undoubtedly the request had been couched in most respectful and diplomatic terms. In writing to the Health Magistracy, however, the Commissioner could let himself go and say openly what he felt. He was a Florentine gentleman speaking to members of his own class; he could express his ideas about priests and processions without reserve – and he did just that: 'These processions are not held by priests through devotional zeal, but rather through their self-interest in taking up a good collection. The priest and his followers then use it in guzzling, as the example of Monte Lupo shows. Each evening, at the expense of the crucifix, they make lavish feasts, and thus, half intoxicated with wine, they then behave insolently, as they did on the evening of the 20th when they removed the whole stockade at the gates of Monte Lupo. . . .' The mere thought of the smashed stockade raised Cavalier Sacchetti's blood pressure by several counts, because he felt the compulsion to add 'if I find whoever did it, they shall not go to the priest for penance.' In other words, if he could identify those scoundrels, he, Commissioner Benedetto Sacchetti, would make them suffer adequately for it and not even give them time to ask for the Lord's forgiveness or to recite the penitential prayers.

That these sentiments found a favourable echo in Florence is evident from the notations that their lordships of the Health Magistracy dictated to their registrar in reply: 'All that [the Commissioner] has ordered is approved as well done; Monsignor the Vicar says he has replied concerning the matter of the priests; in similar occurrences use may be made of the soldiery at Empoli, ordering the sergeant to dispatch the number of soldiers necessary to put down assemblies made against ordinances; he [the Commissioner] may punish those who broke the stockade.' Clearly the State had no intention of abdicating authority.

The bureaucratic machinery was in full action, and those in control were in no humour to slow it down. On Saturday, 26 July, the Commissioner proceeded to interrogate the surgeon and apothecary from the pesthouse – the two men who had organized the serenading of the girl in San

Miniatello on the night of the crimes. The interrogation yielded no new evidence, and the day ended with nothing accomplished.

The 27th was a Sunday, but the Commissioner was obviously in a hurry to conclude the inquiry, and in all probability had other matters in his jurisdiction requiring attention. He still had to interrogate the baker, Antonio di Pavolo Giunti, who had supported the priest against Coveri the Sunday before, and who, according to local rumour, could have been one of those responsible for the breaking of the stockade. In spite of its being Sunday, the Commissioner decided to proceed, and summoned Antonio.

Benedetto Sacchetti knew his business. He began by asking, 'What is your occupation?' 'I am a baker,' replied Antonio. 'Do you own any property, and if so, what?' 'I own certain houses that may be worth 200 *scudi*, and I make 60 or 70 *scudi* in my trade.' The questions had a purpose. Individuals like Antonio who were property-owners could be penalized not only with imprisonment, but also with the confiscation of their possessions. For lower-class people of that period, who were accustomed to a hard life, the confiscation of goods was far more painful than a few 'twists' or a few months in jail or in the galleys. The Commissioner knew how to strike the right note. But the baker was a tough character and showed no signs of being intimidated. His replies during the first part of the interrogation reveal a certain arrogance, and he flatly denied all accusations. At one point, the Commissioner began to lose patience and challenged the baker by saying that, contrary to his assertions, 'It has been established that when those words passed [between the priest and the guards, he, Antonio] was with the priest in order to furnish

67

aid and support if the guards did not leave, having the muskets in order for that purpose, and being armed at the priest's request; and he also argued with Coveri, who had the muskets and other arms at the church removed, and that there were some of his own arms there.' Antonio was unmoved by this barrage and continued his denials: 'I spoke to Coveri only about the suffering in this place and not for any other reason, and it is not true that I was there on the priest's account, or that I had an argument or anything else. I had no other arms than my sword, and a spear that I lent to someone in the procession who said he wanted to make a banner, but I have not done all what your lordship says.'

It was obvious that the baker was lying: all the evidence was against him, but the blusterer had no other way out than to deny everything and proclaim his innocence. The Commissioner moved on to the affair of the stockade with an indirect approach: 'Are you used to staying out at night?' 'I am never out at night.' 'Were you out on the evening of the 20th and 21st?' 'No, I was not.' 'Where do you live?' 'I live there above the inn.' The Commissioner was circling inexorably closer, and finally came to the heart of the matter: 'Do you know that the stockade at the gate has been removed?' In a malicious move to extricate himself from his quandary, the baker had no hesitation in involving poor Pandolfo: 'I have heard that the stockade at the gate was removed, and I understand that Pandolfo said he knew who had removed it.' We cannot say what the Commissioner's private response to this was, but he acted as if it was of little importance, asking: 'Do you know or have you heard who it was that removed the stockade?' The baker kept up his game: 'I have heard nothing.' The Commissioner pressed on: 'Did

A. *Cancelli, et Obices*
B. *Ædicula ex Asseribus pro Commisario*
C. *Ædicula similis pro Militibus.*

Fig. 9 One of the gates of Rome during the epidemic of plague of 1656-7. Note the palisade erected outside the gate

you leave your house on the evening in question when the stockade was removed?' Almost the same question had already been asked twice during the interrogation, and the baker had twice replied with a curt negative. This time, perhaps fearing the Commissioner's insistence, Antonio still stuck to the negative but decided to add some details. Just as he had previously brought Pandolfo into the story, so he now introduced another character of the castello: 'I was in bed,' he said, 'and some young fellows were singing and asked me for something to drink. I got up and, barefoot and in my shirt, gave them something to drink, then I went back inside and they went away; afterwards I saw Giuliano di Antonio Mazzuoli go into his house with a sword or halberd or something of the kind.' Evidently, not many people in Monte Lupo, except women, children, and Pandolfo were in bed and asleep on the night of the misdeeds. At any rate, the Giuliano di Antonio Mazzuoli mentioned by the baker was the same Giuliano who had threatened Pandolfo, telling him not to talk, and so he must have been on the list of suspects. The Commissioner asked 'if the said Giuliano was holding anything else.' The baker answered: 'I did not see anything else.' Clearly, nothing more explicit was to be got out of the baker beyond vague statements disclaiming responsibility. The Commissioner could not refrain from a threat, warning him 'to tell the truth if he did not want to be subjected to a more rigorous examination.' 'I have told the truth,' said the baker, to which the Commissioner retorted: 'Did you retreat [to the church]?' This was an insidious question because the Commissioner evidently knew that the baker, fearing arrest, had gone to the church after the crimes. In the Tuscan courts of the time, to be a 'fugitive' in order to avoid trial was taken as tacit admission of guilt. The people of Tuscany, even in little places like Monte Lupo, were not ignorant of these subtleties of criminal justice, and the baker replied with prudent alacrity: 'I was in church when I was told that the guards wanted to arrest me. I left the church, and I was not a fugitive.'

The interrogation of Antonio Giunti was over, but the suspicions and accusations against him were serious, and the questioning had done nothing to dispel them. While waiting for the Health Magistracy in Florence to pass the final judgement, the baker was 'admonished', and 'since there was no secure prison [in the castello, he] was assigned to his house, which he promised not to leave, even though the door was unlocked, under pain of 300 *scudi*, payable to the Health Magistracy.' Three people in Monte Lupo stood 'security' for the baker in case he should flee.

The conclusion of the interrogation of Antonio is a little puzzling. If the baker was supposed to be imprisoned, why was he not put in jail like poor Pandolfo? If the prison was not secure enough for the baker, why was it regarded as secure for Pandolfo? It might be supposed that there was only one secure place in the prison, that it was already occupied by Pandolfo, and that the Commissioner did not want to put those two characters together. But if that were so, why not state it in the records? Many conjectures are possible, but they remain mere conjectures. The documents give no clues to the puzzle.

On the same Sunday that the Commissioner was questioning the baker, Monsignor the Vicar of the Archbishopric of Florence dispatched a letter to the Commissioner to clarify the official position of the Archbishopric on the misdeeds at Monte Lupo.[23] The letter, written in a silky, involuted style, stated that the Vicar himself, 'supported by the very great devotion of the people of Monte Lupo', had granted permission to the parish priest, Antonio Bontadi to carry out 'the display of the Crucifix', but with severe 'limitations', namely, 'that it was to be an act of only the men of Monte Lupo without the participation of women or of children under twelve, and many other limitations which your lordship may see from my reply to a letter written to me by the aforesaid priest, Antonio, which letter of mine, should you wish to see, I hereby commission him to show you so that your lordship be informed. . . .' Now 'the fact that the said priest over-extended and profited himself much displeases me,' wrote the Vicar, 'and I have given him to understand that he is to obey the order given him [to remain confined to the church and parish house] . . . so that he may perceive his error, since according to your lordship's report, he is deserving of punishment.' No opposition was made to the Commissioner's instituting a judicial inquiry concerning the priest's responsibilities. 'And let your lordship make an informative inquiry while he [the priest] is confined within the limits of his church and parish house'; but by underlining the fact that the inquiry was to be purely 'informative', the Vicar implicitly emphasized that any final judgement was the exclusive concern of ecclesiastical jurisdiction. 'And send me the part [of the inquiry] relating to that priest, Antonio, and you will see that I shall carry out a rigorous prosecution against him and, through his example, against others subject to this ecclesiastical court.' As the Commissioner had 'confined the priest to his house under penalty of 300 *scudi* payable to the

71

Treasury' [i.e. reverting to the State], the Vicar raised an objection, but in a smooth, sanctimonious tone, pretending to believe that it was not an oversight on the part of the Commissioner but on the part of his registrar. 'Let your lordship advise the notary who in your name drafted that order that the fine is not properly allocated, and it should be stated that it is to be applied to poor monasteries or other religious institutions.' In other words, according to Monsignor the Vicar, the State could impose a fine of 300 *scudi* if the priest did not observe the restriction, but in that event the sum was to go not to the State but to the benefit of 'poor monasteries or other religious institutions'. With respect to the danger foreseen by the Commissioner that 'similar observances and processions may be made by other curates and priests', the Vicar felt sure that 'they cannot do so without permission, nor do I believe they would be so daring, and I have no wish to allow it.' The letter concluded sanctimoniously: 'Let your mind be tranquil, and should you have cause [for concern], dexterously and with your mercy and prudence let them [the priests of the villages] know that they should desist [from organizing processions] unless they have permission from us here, and we shall act cautiously when considering every request made.'

In all probability Sacchetti did not stay in Monte Lupo in the days following the interrogation of the baker. Troubles and problems were springing up like mushrooms in every corner of the district under his jurisdiction. In Empoli 'daily new cases of infection are discovered.' Poggibonsi 'had become a sink of iniquity. They refused to admit the officers of the law, they beat them and sent them packing, and came near to making difficulties for the corporal . . . they think they can treat me as they

72

have their Mayor, whom they have made do as they please.'[24] Benedetto Sacchetti had no lack of cats to skin, but Monte Lupo remained at the top of his list: he sent soldiers from Empoli to control the scoundrels there, and on 9 August, he himself was back in the castello to conduct a new interrogation of Pandolfo. The poor fellow had spent seventeen long days in prison. When the Commissioner saw him brought in again by the guards, he went straight to the point, but not without a suggestion of irony which Pandolfo must have found anything but amusing: 'Had the prison made him resolve to tell the truth about who the people were who had removed the stockade at the gate of Monte Lupo?' Jail must have been an unpleasant experience, because Pandolfo, although continuing to deny having recognized the malefactors in the dark, did 'resolve' to tell things that he had hitherto refused to disclose. 'I did not recognize them,' he declared; 'I can tell you that I saw Master Giuliano Mazzuoli, the carpenter, sawing a plank from the stockade at the gate one morning three or four days before the stockade was actually removed. And this plank he brought to my house; and I also saw Caterina, wife of Giovanni the mason, who today has the plague, and Rosa, wife of Francesco, called the Chicken (*il Pollo*). And the said Master Giuliano asked me to say nothing.' This was the third time that the name of the carpenter, Giuliano Mazzuoli, had been mentioned in the different interrogations, and the Commissioner asked: 'Why did he tell you to say nothing?' 'I don't know,' replied Pandolfo, 'but he told me then to say nothing.' 'Why did Master Mazzuoli remove a plank?' insisted the Commissioner. 'I don't know,' answered Pandolfo.

It was clear that no useful information was to be

73

extracted by continuing in this direction, but with almost obsessive pertinacity the Commissioner repeated for the nth time the question, 'Who were the men then who actually did destroy the stockade?' For the nth time, Pandolfo replied: 'I did not recognize them.' The Commissioner tried to pin Pandolfo down: 'But you did recognize them because you told the surgeon and the apothecary that you would swear it was not they – which indicates that you know who it really was.' The reply was candid: 'I told them it was not they, because if it had been, I should have recognized them.'

Obviously it was impossible to bring the matter to a head. Pandolfo was 'warned to tell the truth unless he wanted to be subject to a more rigorous examination.' This was an explicit and disturbing threat. The 'more rigorous examination' could be torture or something similar. Pandolfo was unmoved: 'I did not recognize them. I don't know who they were. Do what you will.' Unable to extract useful information and justifying his decision with the 'consideration that imprisonment had been sufficient punishment', Commissioner Sacchetti sent Pandolfo home. The mystery of who had destroyed the stockade remained unsolved.

V

THE INQUIRY into the crimes in Monte Lupo followed two distinctly different routes. On one side was the attempt to establish exactly how the misdeeds had occurred and to identify those responsible for them. This was the purpose of the interrogations which have been reported in detail in the preceding pages. But that was only part of the inquiry. At the same time a serious attempt was made to establish the consequences of the disturbances on the course of the epidemic, with the idea of evaluating the final degree of responsibility of the culprits. If this second line of inquiry did not produce the local colour and folklore that are revealed by the interrogations, it is certainly of far greater importance from the standpoint of the history of epidemiology.

We get a first glimpse of it in the report made by the corporal of the guards, Antonio Chiatti, to Commissioner Sacchetti on 23 July. The corporal stated thus:

By means of these processions and gatherings it is feared that some new attack of the plague has been caused, because we found [that] in Monte Lupo a daughter of Bastiano the carter, in Sanmontana two or three [persons], in Limite two, in Fibbiana two more – all [became infected] with the plague, [since the day of the procession] up until now, the 23rd [of July].

The fact that a man of humble birth and little or no education such as Corporal Chiatti could relate processions to the spread of disease, completely free from religious preoccupations, throws a significant light on ways of thought that had been gradually gaining ground since the end of the Middle Ages and by the seventeenth century had reached even the lower levels of the population. If a guard corporal could argue in this way, it is not surprising that among the high officials of the Health Department ideas prevailed that did not please the clergy.

Commissioner Sacchetti's report of 25 July to the Health Magistracy of Florence has already been mentioned; on the basis of testimonies made by Corporal Chiatti on 23 July, and probably on reports by Father Dragoni as well, the Commissioner wrote that: 'As a result, the disease which seemed checked [reappeared] after that day, [and] among the people who came to the ceremony [the procession] we found that several [became] infected who were taken to the pesthouse, most of them were women.'

It is highly significant that the Health Authority felt the need to support such statements by concrete facts. Among the papers still preserved in the archive of the Health Magistracy are two highly significant documents. One is the *List of all those who became ill after the procession that took place in Monte Lupo on 20 and 21 July, 1631.*[1] This document records the cases of plague found by the health service in Monte Lupo and in seven other neighbouring communities in the period from 21 July, the day following the procession on the Sunday, until 8 August – 19 days in all. The places listed besides Monte Lupo are those from which the inhabitants came to join in the procession at the castello. The *List* indicates in each case the date on which the disease was reported and the name of the patient; in fifteen cases out of 50 the age is noted, and in three other cases a general indication of age is given (boy or girl); when members of the same family appear, the document mentions the degree of relationship. The basic data derivable from the *List* (excluding names, age, and relationship) are tabulated in the table on p. 86.

The other document, dated 15 August, 1631, is a report from the health deputies in San Miniatello; this report mentions the names of all the inhabitants of the village who took part 'in the display of the most Holy Crucifix made in Monte Lupo on the 20th of July.'[2] The report gives the names and relationships of 40 males and 56 females 'aged 12 and over'. We cannot say for certain whether reports similar to this one from San Miniatello were requested from the other villages; it is also possible that such reports were compiled but have since been lost. The method of compilation of the San Miniatello report, where two zeros are marked against the categories of boys and girls 'under 12', suggests that a precise questionnaire was circulated among the communities by order of Commissioner Sacchetti or the Florentine health authorities. In any case, the procedure followed by the health officials is obvious and clearly corresponds to the rules for modern epidemiological research. On one hand, an attempt was made to identify the people who took part in the procession and their possible contacts. On the other, fresh cases of infection were noted, with precise identification of the patients and their degree of relationship. By linking the two things, the authorities tried to ascertain whether the procession had produced a revival of the epidemic. At that time, no one knew exactly how long the incubation period for the plague was. The investigation of new cases extended over the period of 19 days following the proces-

77

sion of 20 July. The short quarantine was 22 days (cf. Appendix), and the inquiry was presumably based on that concept.

Today we know that the period of incubation for bubonic plague is generally from two to seven days, and for pulmonary plague from one to three days. On this basis, the striking fact (cf. table on p. 86) is that the cases of disease reported on 25, 26, and 27 July (the fifth, sixth, and seventh days respectively after the procession of the 20th – and we should remember that there was a second procession on 21 July) represent 34 per cent of all the cases reported for the entire period, while the three days in question are only 16 per cent of the total number of days considered. In other words, there actually was a concentration of new cases of infection in the critical days after the procession. The immediate conclusion would seem to be that the health officials were right when they asserted that the processions triggered a worsening of the epidemic. However, almost half the cases for 25, 26, and 27 July came from one single village – Limite, and we have no way of knowing if the people who died of plague in Limite during those days had actually attended the processions. That leaves the possibility of analyzing the roster for the village of San Miniatello, for which we have not only the record of new cases of infection, but also the list of those who took part in the procession of 20 July. Of the four individuals who became sick with the plague in San Miniatello during the period in question, at least one – and possibly two – took part in the ceremony.[3] At first glance, this fact seems to corroborate the health officials' opinion, but again a closer look gives rise to a certain scepticism. The number of people from San Miniatello in the procession was 96, and the one or two

78

cases of reported illness represent a decidedly low percentage. Moreover, those two cases did not occur until nine or fourteen days respectively after the procession. An incubation period of nine or fourteen days is not impossible, but it is longer than normal.

In conclusion, on the basis of the data available, it is not possible to say that Don Antonio Bontadi's initiative had effectively rekindled the epidemic. The health officials of the time, however, had no doubts; according to their computation, in the nineteen days they investigated, out of a total of 50 new cases, the women outnumbered the men 28 to 22. As there were more women than men in the processions, the correlation proved – so the officials argued – that the processions aggravated the contagion. It was a very crude and primitive way of handling statistics and extracting causal relationships from them. Paradoxically, the health officials were mistaken, though they were on the right track, while the priest, Don Antonio Bontadi, was right even though he was on the wrong one.

The fact that the processions did not cause a recrudescence of the epidemic was not a miracle of the Crucifix. The normal sequence of contagion in cases of bubonic plague is from rat to rat's flea (*Xenopsylla cheopsis*) to man. Recent epidemiological and bacteriological researches have proved that the human flea, *Pulex irritans,* can compensate by numbers for its low individual efficiency as carrier of the bacillus, *Yersinia pestis,* so that in socioeconomic conditions where there is widespread ecto-parasitism the sequence man → man's flea → man cannot be excluded. On the other hand, if pulmonary complications develop in patients afflicted with the plague, then direct interhuman contagion, i.e. the sequence man → man) is also possible.

If the disorders that took place in Monte Lupo did not cause a revival of the epidemic, the explanation is that (a) the sequence rat → rat's flea → man remains the most frequent and probable method of spreading the plague; (b) in all probability the epizootic that was basic to the epidemic was in the process of dying out. In the verdict of history these considerations may absolve the priest, Don Bontadi from the accusation of having provoked new deaths with his daring initiative. But this does not justify the priest. In view of the possibility of the sequence man → man's flea → man, or of the outbreak of cases of pneumonic plague, the health officials – though totally ignorant of bacteriological technicalities – were perfectly in the right when they sought to prevent assemblies of people.

VI

THE LAST death caused by the plague in Monte Lupo
occurred on 11 August, just a few days after the epidemiological inquiry described above had been completed. One
more case presumed to be of plague was reported on 25
August, but it was not fatal. In Monte Lupo the epidemic
was over.

The balance sheet of the epidemic was tragic. As Father
Dragoni put it: 'A large part [of the people] are dead,
the rest are ruined or quarantined. There are plenty of
debts. No one is to be found who will make loans or give
credit.' The taxes were collected with difficulty, 'he who
can pay makes more trouble than the poor man.'[1] And
the troubles were not over. The plague no longer afflicted
the Castello, but it continued to pervade the surrounding
countryside.

By order of the Health Magistracy, the pesthouse outside the castello walls was kept open to receive the sick
of the district. 'The neighbourhood is large,' commented
Father Dragoni, 'and if one place does not supply us
another does, and infected persons come from up to ten
miles away to this hospital.' The supervision of the
lazaretto remained in Father Dragoni's care, and for him
it was a continuous source of problems – or 'vexations',
as he liked to call them. Funds were unfailingly inadequate. 'There are many debts, and I remain creditor for
a good sum,' he wrote on 23 August, and added: 'I have

sold my grain and harvest at a loss in order to meet the daily expenses. Now I no longer know where to turn.' On 8 October he reiterated: 'We are 50 *scudi* in debt to the baker and to the man who has given us wine.' The people who should have been his collaborators made endless trouble for him. On 12 September the Father reported to the Health Magistracy that he had been 'forced to evict the apothecary from the pesthouse and lock him up in a house, because he played cards and had dealings with everyone indiscriminately, and I discovered that he introduced women from Monte Lupo into the pesthouse to eat and drink and at night to sleep with him. And besides, he would go out at night and with several inn-keepers would go to fetch wine in the Chianti area, in spite of the edict against leaving the district.' The soldiers that Commissioner Sacchetti had transferred from Empoli to Monte Lupo to control the people in the castello proved to be ruffians of the worst sort, and the source of more tribulation than help. Father Dragoni reported to Florence that they were 'disorderly and insolent; they form squadrons and go around at night with forbidden arms such as halberds, etc. They have insulted the health officers, particularly the surgeon, and threatened to lay out my registrar, who has served me nearly a year in that office; similarly they have not respected my own person, an elderly sexagenarian with no other arms to defend myself than my breviary and rosary.' As if this were not enough, the monk continued to be harassed by the Monte Lupans on account of his position and the restrictions and burdens it stood for. On 8 October, at his wits' end, the Father wrote to Florence that 'I am very anxious to be allowed to come to the city and to be freed once and for all from this responsibility which I have discharged at the cost of many vexations.'²

On 25 October the Health Magistracy authorized the removal of the stockade, and the people and merchandise of Monte Lupo were finally granted 'the possibility of coming to Florence', on the specific condition that they carry health passes.³ The responsibility for the passes was naturally entrusted to Father Dragoni, who had already warned Florence on 7 November that 'there are many false passes in use, and some people are making them as a trade and business.' He had seized many forged passes, he wrote, and not to mince matters, he characteristically added, 'and to speak freely, some priests have been infringing the edicts and laws of the Magistracy.' Having shot that bolt, the Father launched into a precise account of his work:

I have not acted unjustly and have accompanied severity with compassion and charity. . . . I have directed and fed two pest-houses, convalescents, servants; I have paid guards and grave-diggers with the alms your lordships have sent me. I reduced the necessary expenses to a minimum and removed the superfluous. There remains a debt of about 100 *scudi*, part of which is due to me and part to bakers and others. I will satisfy everyone and settle my own accounts.⁴

The typical traits of Father Dragoni's character are all fully present in this passage: honesty and precision, but with an extremely high opinion of himself and of his own worth. He insisted on his Christian and 'charitable' disposition, but in fact he was unfailingly highly critical of others. His references to the work of the late Mayor Francesco della Stufa, who had taken his place as head of the Health Office from the beginning of April until the beginning of June, are totally lacking in generosity:

83

In more than a year that I have held this office, no one has died without sacrament or confession (may this be said to the honour and glory of God's Majesty), whereas during the month when I retired and the Mayor of blessed memory was in charge, about 200 persons died without confession or other sacraments.[5]

And in another letter a few days later:

Many debts have come to light, left by Mayor della Stufa, of blessed memory, in the short time that he was in charge, which was a month or a little more. The accounts for his administration have never been seen, because immediately after his death his heirs had his writings and all other materials taken away. I was not in office at that time, and I have no record of his administration, and the creditors are coming to me.[6]

Francesco della Stufa had not been a great success. But if many people had died in the pesthouse unconfessed, and if the debts had increased, this was the result of the generosity with which della Stufa had admitted the sick from the countryside to the hospital – a policy that was in accordance with the directives from the Magistracy in Florence.

Father Dragoni was the kind of man who can make himself respected but not loved. Least of all was he loved by Monte Lupo's priest, Don Antonio Bontadi, who, when referring to him in his parish book, did not call him 'Reverend Father Dragoni' or even 'Father Dragoni', but simply and acidly as 'Il Dragoni.'

Don Antonio was possibly reprimanded for his ill-judged behaviour and for having caused so much confusion in the castello. But he was allowed to keep his position and died in Monte Lupo on 16 January, 1661, at the age of 59.[7]

Little is known about Commissioner Sacchetti after the

84

middle of August. He fell ill in the autumn, and his place was taken by another Florentine gentleman, from the noble family of Capponi. Sacchetti's illness was not the plague, but it must have been equally serious as he died in the following year, 1632.[8]

The surgeon, Coveri, continued to travel from one city to another, from one village to another, making inspections, bringing instructions, sending meticulous reports back to Florence, and on every possible occasion irritating people by his disputatious and aggressive manner.

The other characters in our tale vanish into the mists of history. Perhaps in some dark corner of the state archives in Florence there may still be the final records of the proceedings begun by Commissioner Sacchetti, complete with the final verdict and consequent penalties. But the author of these pages has not succeeded in finding them.

Who broke down the stockade at Monte Lupo? Was Pandolfo lying when he swore he had not recognized the evildoers? And what role was played by the carpenter, Giuliano Mazzuoli and the baker, Antonio di Pavolo Giunti in the whole affair? These are questions that must remain unanswered. The reader may be disappointed, and if so, the author offers his apologies. But indeed this book was not written to answer these questions, but rather to recapture emotions, attitudes and behaviour of all segments of a society in a period distant in many ways from our own, yet where the germination of modern thought had already begun.

CASES OF PLAGUE REPORTED IN MONTE LUPO AND THE SURROUNDING COMMUNITIES BETWEEN JULY 21 AND AUGUST 8, 1631

	Monte Lupo		S. Quirico		Fabbiana		Samontana		S. Miniatello		Capraia		Castellina		Limite		Totals		
July	M	F	M	F	M	F	M	F	M	F	M	F	M	F	M	F	M	F	M&F
21		1													1		1	1	2
22						1												1	1
23						1												1	1
24								1										1	1
25					1	2											1	2	3
26		1				1									5	3	5	5	10
27	3								1								4		4
28												1						1	1
29					1					1							1	1	2
30				1					1	1							1	2	3
31	1												1	1			2	1	3
August																			
1			2			1								1			2	2	4
2					2	1											2	1	3
3	1	2															1	2	3
4		1			1	3											1	4	5
5							1										1		1
6		1																1	1
7				1														1	1
8		1																1	1
Totals	5	7	2	2	5	10	1	1	2	2		1	1	2	6	3	22	28	50

Appendix I

INSTRUCTIONS OF THE MAGISTRACY OF HEALTH IN FLORENCE FOR JUSTICES IN THE COUNTRYSIDE

In 1630, when the plague epidemic was raging, the central administration of the Grand Duchy of Tuscany printed: 'The Instructions of the Health Board of Florence for the Justices in the countryside in case of infectious sicknesses that might be discovered in the areas under their jurisdiction.'* These *Istruzioni* were to serve as a guide for the local administrators in the countryside in fighting the plague.

'It being the task of all justices, criminal as well as civil, to watch over everything that concerns good government, they shall in particular, above all else, have an eye to good regulations regarding the interests of the Public Health, and for this purpose shall make shift to have notice of all cases of sickness believed to be infectious that should chance to occur in their jurisdictions and as soon as they come by news of any case whether of sickness or death, they shall observe the following and proceed to carry out the orders herein described against any persons whatsoever, even if they should be Florentine citizens or others in other ways privileged.

* A copy of these *'Istruzioni'* is preserved in ASF Sanità, Bandi t. 2, c. 64.

'First, they shall give orders to whomever is concerned that those dead of suspected plague are not to be buried in the churches but in the countryside far from the high roads, and a hundred armslengths from the houses, and in a grave at least three armslengths deep with the benediction that will seem fit to the priests of the parish church where such deaths may be, and if there are no gravediggers, have the corpse put on a ladder and handling it as little as possible, carried to the grave, and, where possible, put on the said corpse lime and then earth.

'As soon as the news arrives of the sickness being discovered in whatsoever house, the Justice shall give orders that the sick man be carried to the pesthouse, if it is near enough for him to be carried there.

'Then he will have orders given to the occupants of the house where the sickness has been, if they are tenants, that they must not leave the house and the fields where they are, that they must not associate with anybody, and must not give away anything from their house or fields under pain, as transgressors, of their lives and confiscation of their goods.

'If the sick of the said houses should be far from the pesthouses so that they could not with ease be carried thither, give in any case orders that none must leave home or fields, as above, being tenants.

'If the said sick are subtenants or live in houses without land the order must be given to all the occupants, with the said penalty, not to leave the house.

'As the said persons under orders need to be sustained with victuals, if they are tenants, give orders to the owners of the land that they supply the said victuals, giving them credit to repay at the harvests or in some other way.

'If they are farmworkers, or occupants of houses without land, or poor, give order to the Chamberlain of the Council that he supply them with the necessary victuals from some innkeeper or shopkeeper nearby to the amount of eight *soldi* a day per head.

'If the landlords of the said sick tenants should not live in the same jurisdiction so that the order cannot be given to them, then have the Chamberlain of the Council supply the said expenses for victuals for the said eight *soldi* a day for each one of those under orders as above.

'And they shall give orders that the victuals be brought to those under orders, not in money, but in bread and eatables by the nearest innkeepers or shopkeepers or others they deem suitable, and such things should be delivered through the windows or in some other way such that whoever brings them does not approach and does not converse with the suspect cases and those under orders, and for this debt they must be reimbursed by the owners of the land who in turn shall reimburse themselves from the peasants on whom the money is being spent.

'The said Justices will give order to the Health Deputies nearest the dwelling of the suspects, or to other of their officials, who will from time to time go and inspect the affected areas and ensure that victuals are supplied them as above and that they do not leave the house and land respectively assigned to them as the place of disinfection, which they must do, proceeding against transgressors with every rigour, having them isolated and the doors of their houses nailed up; and then after the usual disinfection have them put into prison and advise the Magistrate of the Health Board of Florence and await orders from him, which will be given.

'The quarantine and disinfection that are to be carried out in each house must be of twenty-two days at least from the day that the last person sick with the suspect sickness had died or recovered; after this period the said houses can be opened and freed.

'It must be noted that before the houses closed or under orders are opened even where none of the occupants is left, it is very fitting and necessary that first the said houses be perfumed and purified in the following manner and with the diligence described, to wit:

'First, whoever enters the house to perfume it should carry in his hand brushwood, or something like it, lighted and burning and should go upstairs with it and make fire with flames in the rooms. Then shut the windows tight and make smoke with sulphur all through the house.

'Sweep the floors, benches, and walls well, and if possible, whitewash the house or, at least, wash the walls down with alkaline solution using a whitewashing brush. The woodwork should also be washed down with alkaline solution. Put the linen cloths to soak in water and wash the mattresses and put other cloths where they can get air, and keep them aired for many, many days before they are used again. And those that were used directly by the infected person are to be burnt if they be woollens or linen. The room where the dead or sick person had been must, for three days after it has come empty, be washed out with vinegar, and have it swept thoroughly every day, and the first time, scatter lime around the room and throw vinegar over it until it has smoked and burnt itself out.

'And since it often chances that the sick are peasants far away from lands and castles and from the advantage of being able to have physicians and medicines, make very sure that they know of some easy medicines proposed to the Magistrates of the Health Board as being easy by their physicians, with which the occupants of the said houses under orders and the sick themselves may make their own medicines.

'And they shall do their utmost to save those, above all, who are healthy in the said closed houses; and for this purpose the latter, every morning, shall take some Venice treacle, oil themselves with oil against the poison, and other like preservatives, and if they have none of these, shall take nuts, and dried figs, and rue and, early in the morning, eat them or other things that are meant for the purpose.

'Every morning the sick shall take a five-ounce glass of very hot chick-pea or goat's-rue juice, and shall cover themselves well so as to sweat; they must be informed that sweating is an excellent remedy for the infectious sickness that is latent. That they strive to bring out this sweat, however, with fire or with putting cloths on or as best they can.

'Oil the swellings that appear with oil of white lilies or of camomile or flax seeds and place upon them a little wool soaked in one of these oils.

'If these swellings do not come out, go about to make them do so with a cupping glass or by putting on them white onion roasted on the embers and mixed with Venice treacle.

'If a blister or small carbuncle be found, put upon it devil's bit or scabious grass crushed between two stones, and, to remove the scab, put a little chicken fat on it and slit with a razor and then put a little Venice treacle on it. Around the small carbuncle put pomegranate juice together with the pomegranate seeds, well peeled and crushed together.

'The sick must take good care of themselves, eating meat, eggs, and good things; they must abstain from wine, and drink boiled water with the soft part of a loaf and a few coriander seeds in it.

'Note must be taken of these medicines for the use of those who cannot have, as above, the services of physicians or other medicines, those, that is, like the poor peasants who live in the countryside, etc.'

Appendix 2

Towards the end of June 1631, the Magistracy of Public Health in Florence made arrangements to select five new Commissioners-General who would represent them in the five districts into which the Florentine territory was subdivided. The letter notifying the five Florentine noblemen of their selection gives a clear idea of the authority and responsibilities connected with the position of Commissioner-General.* It therefore seems appropriate to reproduce the complete text of the letter in this appendix:

'Our experience, already too long, of the ill effects of the contagious disease which has afflicted our city for so many months, and which now makes itself felt in many territories, castelli, and districts of our State, teaches and makes plain to us that any spread and increase of that disease arises for the most part from the people's disobedience and lack of observance of the proper ordinances which have been generally issued. For this reason we think it necessary to appoint five gentlemen who, as Commissioners of Health, shall go out to different districts, and by virtue of their supreme authority shall make known by just and severe penalties how futile and pernicious it is to transgress [the law], and how profitable it is to bow

* A copy of the letter is preserved in ASF Sanità, Copialettere, b. 58, cc. 52–54 (29 June 1631).

93

to the will of superiors who with reason and sound judgement make the decrees, and as one of these five, you,
Signor ————, have been selected as a person known
to His Serene Highness, our Lord [Duke], and to this
Magistracy, as being most fit for such great responsibility
and as having the knowledge and ability wholly to accom-
plish through your prudence that which is necessary and
desired, and this is given into your charge and under your
jurisdiction.

'You shall transport yourself as soon as possible to those
districts in order to initiate the duties of the office assigned
to you, and, ourselves desiring to facilitate in part that
task of yours, we have decided to send these present
instructions with you.

'First of all, you must remember that your authority is
supreme, as you may see from the letters patent that His
Serene Highness has been pleased to grant you, and from
the edict drawn up by us, also by order of His Highness,
and that therefore you shall exercise it with the care and
discretion that shall seem fitting to you, having nevertheless this particular end in view, namely, that your authority
be recognized, respected, and feared by all.

'You shall have in your train a Registrar selected by
you, who shall be a notary and shall have some experience
of criminal cases, and to whom you shall give the expenses
for food, and he is to serve in drawing up reports of the
interrogations that are made of accused persons and witnesses, and to take note of the charges against each and
of what may appear in excuse; and the decisions and
sentences that are to be carried out by your orders, without, however, formally holding trials; and to write letters
and do anything else that occurs to you.

'There shall also be assigned to you a Corporal with

94

more guards, who is to attend you on your travels, and through whom the orders you issue may be carried out, it being also possible for you to avail yourself of local officers by the authority granted you in your letters patent.

'On your arrival in any territory or castello in your jurisdiction where there may be a suitable number of inhabitants, in order that your authority and the more general and important ordinances to be observed may be made known to all, you shall with a trumpet sound publish by a town crier, messenger, or other person the edict that you have brought from the Magistracy, and you shall leave a printed copy of that edict posted where you think it will be best seen and read by the inhabitants of that place, with orders that it is to be removed by no one. At your side you shall have the deputies of Public Health for each locality, and where there are no deputies, the representatives of the populace or other persons, from whom you shall diligently gather information concerning the circumstances that both have accompanied and still do accompany the aforesaid disease, not only in that place, but also in neighbouring places, what ordinances have been and are being observed, what disorders are in need of remedy, also the opinion of the deputies and others concerning the remedies they proposed; and then being thus well informed, you shall establish such ordinances as you deem necessary.

'You shall set up your residence in the place most convenient for keeping informed about every part of your jurisdiction, and you shall not fail to make the rounds often, to ascertain in person what is happening in those places.

'Where you know that the disease is prevalent, you shall order pesthouses to be set up, always outside walled towns,

95

and in places where they may serve other neighbouring people who may have need of them.

'The care of organizing such pesthouses and the management of them you shall commit to the deputies of Public Health, or to others whom you deem more suitable.

'Expenses: if they can be arranged by means of voluntary contributions from the populace, as has been done in many places, it would be very appropriate; otherwise, you shall have the money that is immediately necessary disbursed by the Treasury of the city, Mayoral district, or Vicarate, and according as you advise, we shall lend as much as may be needed.

'If the places lack doctors or surgeons and there are such in the district who are not busy, you shall give them orders and summons to come and serve, having the local representatives assign them suitable provision for lodging, and these men, while appointed by your order, shall be approved by us, and, if there is difficulty in finding doctors or surgeons, you are to advise us.

'You shall also see that the ordinance is observed whereby the inhabitants of houses where contagious illness has been discovered shall be locked in, allowing, however, farmers to go to their farms without observing this, and that all lodgers and poor people who need it shall be given victuals at the rate of eight *soldi* per day per head, and that this expense be borne by the Treasurers of the place, and if they are unable, let the deputies of Public Health cause the victuals to be provided by the shopkeepers, innkeepers, or whoever is able to do it, so that those shut in their houses shall have no reason to go out.

'Similarly in places where you may forbid, by means of the above-mentioned edict or otherwise, anyone to leave his district, you shall arrange that the necessary things be provided by having what is needed brought to the boundary of that district and delivered with such caution as may be necessary for the safety of him who makes the delivery.

'You shall make the deputies of Public Health responsible for seeing that the gravediggers take from infected houses the clothes and bedding used by the sick, or that they burn them and have the houses purified by fires, sulphur and calcine, accordingly as the method for effecting such purification specifies.

'In places where there has been little disease and where it has been unnecessary to establish pesthouses, you shall see to it that the ecclesiastical authorities provide gravediggers and that it shall be their business to have the houses fumigated, and, if they are unwilling to undertake such a task, you shall assign it to some other person in the place whom you deem to be more suitable; the Magistracy customarily pays the gravediggers five *scudi* a month each.

'You shall cause to be observed faithfully everywhere that which is set down in the printed edict delivered to you and which you shall have proclaimed as stated above, as shall also be observed all other ordinances issued by our Magistracy that pertain particularly to more specific places, and therefore you shall inform all Officers of Justice and other Commissioners authorized by the Magistracy of Public Health by our letters patent beyond the ten mile [limit] of said orders that they hold from us, so that you may command the obedience of the populace, and those Commissioners are to carry out their duty under your supervision.

'And if these ordinances that have been or may on occasion be issued by this Magistracy, seem to you to benefit by being revoked or altered because of changing times or because we were misinformed, then you shall advise us of this in your letters, specifying the reason that inclines you to revocation or change, so that with your being in the district and therefore better able to understand the circumstances there obtaining, we may with your opinion ever apply ourselves to reaching better decisions.

'You shall not fail to take care that in the places under your jurisdiction good bread be made, and that other edible material is not of such poor quality as to increase the contagious disease.

'If the orders issued to date both by the aforementioned edict and by any other special ordinance, do not seem sufficient for the security and safety that is desired, you being in the place shall be able to make new ordinances and decisions and have these proclaimed and observed as you think fit; and, so that we may be kept informed, you shall advise us of what you have ordered and laid down, just as in other important circumstances that may arise from time to time you shall also advise us of the ordinance, which places should not have commerce with the city of Florence, which of those places that until now have been forbidden such commerce and where it is time to restore it, to the end that we do not have commerce with those we should not, and do not forbid it to those to whom it should not be forbidden; similarly when it is time to lift the ban from the places that are closed and may not trade with others; and being confident that you will be able to take all necessary measures in your prudence, and trusting in that [prudence] in all other matters that may arise, we shall add no more. God be with you.'

Appendix 3

The *Libro dei Morti di S. Giovanni Evangelista a Monte Lupo* (Book of the Dead for the Parish of St John the Evangelist in Monte Lupo) is preserved in the Archives of the Archiepiscopal Court in Florence. The book covers the period 1629–1839, and, as the title page informs us, it was begun 'in the time of the Reverend M. Antonio Bontadi, Prior of S. Giovanni Evangelista in Monte Lupo, Anno Domini 1629.'

From 3 March to 11 October, 1630, the following deaths are registered: *

Date	Sex	Age	Place of death or Residence
March 3	F		
August 26	F	25	Monte Lupo
September 1	F*	25	Inn outside [the gate]
September 16	M*	12	
September 16	F	58	
September 20	F	35	
September 28	F*		Inn outside [the gate]
September 29	F*	18	
October 1	F*	48	Inn outside [the gate]
October 2	M	13	Monte Lupo
October 3	F	60	Monte Lupo

* I have marked with an asterisk the dead belonging to the family of Aurelio Mostardini, who kept the inn outside the gate where the plague was first detected.

99

October 4	F	35	Monte Lupo
October 4	F	18	
October 5	F	45	
October 5	M	13	
October 5	F	18	
October 5	F	16	
October 6	M*	12	Inn outside [the gate]
October 8	F	50	
October 10	F	30	
October 11	F	30	
October 11	M	40	
October 11	F	13	

The *Libro dei Morti* also indicates the place of burial for each of the deceased. Until 6 October 1630, the dead were buried in the regular graveyards of Monte Lupo or San Miniatello. Caterina di Antonio Palloni, who died on 8 October, 'was the first to be buried in Cacciacane', and those who died on subsequent days were all buried 'in Cacciacane'. The reason for this is that when an epidemic was recognized as such the authorities were not only concerned with opening a pesthouse to isolate the sick, but they also hastened to establish a new cemetery far from where people lived; this was because they feared that the decomposing bodies of those dead of the plague would give rise to miasmas that could spread the infection as they were exuded from the ground.

The pesthouse was opened on 11 October. When people there were dying, they received the sacraments from a member of the clergy attached to the pesthouse – usually a friar – and the matter was considered to be outside the jurisdiction of the parish priest. It was therefore normal that deaths occurring in hospitals were not recorded in parish registers, but in special books at the hospitals themselves. In addition, those who died of plague in their homes were not normally recorded in the parish registers, as infected people were usually confessed and given the sacraments not by the parish priests but by the friars who served in the pesthouses.

Monsignor Bontadi put his *Libro dei Morti* away in a drawer on 11 October. He took it out again on 22 October, when a young man, aged 22, 'at his home passed to a better life.' Once Don Antonio had the book out, he could not refrain from setting down a record of the epidemic:

On the 11th day of October the people of the castello of Monte Lupo who were pronounced sick of the contagion and plague, *que omnia Dei misericordia absint,* began to occupy the pesthouse set up for that purpose by the men and mayoralty of Monte Lupo in a place called the Tall House, the property of Canon Petrucci, in the parish of San Miniatello, where at this date, 22 October, 1630, there are about 28 persons, male and female.

The land which was to have been used for the Sacristy for the Oratory of Cacciacane, likewise in the parish of San Miniatello, was designated as burial ground and cemetery. And this was in the time of the Rev. Mons. Antonio Bontadi of St. Pietro in Bagno, presently Prior of St. Giovanni Evangelista in Monte Lupo, who until now, *Dei maxime misericordia,* has been preserved from this contagion. For the memory of posterity.

Don Antonio put the book back in the drawer. He took it out again a little more than three months later, on 2 February 1631, but not to register the dead. The Arno had overflowed its banks in an unusual manner, and Don Antonio wanted to record this too 'for the memory of posterity': On the 2nd day of February, today, Sunday, there was a flood of water so great that the whole plain from Empoli to here was seen to be under water, and people came by boat along the road and through Monte Lupo.

The registration of the dead was resumed on 1 March 1631, when a young man of 28 died. He was 'from Scarperia, a soldier of war, who returned here sick to the inn inside the castello, where he passed to a better life; he was buried in San Carlo, not being suspected of the plague.'

As stated in the preceding pages, the epidemic seemed to be over in Monte Lupo by the end of February, and the pesthouse was closed during March. Monsignor Bontadi therefore resumed the regular registrations. A week after the soldier's death, a twelve-year-old girl died on 8 March, and on 6 May, a little girl of five. Then the plague broke out again. People died of it in the castello in both April and May, and, for the reason mentioned above, Don Antonio did not record these deaths. But considering the importance of the event, on 4 June he did register the death of Mayor della Stufa, who in all probability died in the Mayoral *Palazzo,* but 'having died of the contagious disease' was buried in Cacciacane. Don Antonio again put his book away, and did not take it out again until 18 August when, as mentioned earlier, the epidemic was practically over.

The deaths appearing in Don Antonio's records for the following months have the typical pattern of post-epidemic mortality. Initially, deaths are very infrequent because the survivors were few, and those few were obviously tough. Then the number of deaths increases, but the deaths are mainly of babies, and this fact reflects both the natural demographic recovery after the catastrophe and the prevalent high levels of infant mortality. The general picture is what one might expect. But there is one somewhat doubtful point. Is it possible that between August 1631 and August 1632 only two deaths occurred in the castello? Were there cases of death that Don Antonio did not register? The regularity of the registration might have suffered if Don Antonio had been temporarily relieved from his duty during the inquiry into the turmoil that had occurred in July in Monte Lupo. We do not know. One thing is certain: although Don Antonio entered in his *Libro dei Morti* 'for the memory of posterity' notes about the plague and the flood and about a child who, having been entrusted to Father Dragoni, died without being given the sacraments, he never bothered to enter in his book 'for the memory of posterity' mention of the disturbances instigated by himself and the reprimands that followed.

Bibliography

BATTISTINI, M., *Le epidemie in Volterra dal 1004 al 1800*, Volterra, 1916.

BIAGETTI, L., 'I Cappuccini nella peste della Toscana degli anni 1630', 31, 33, in *Eco di S. Francesco* 2. 1884.

CATELLACCI, D. (ed.), 'Curiosi ricordi del contagio di Firenze del 1630', in *Archivo Storico Italiano*, ser 5, vol 20. 1897.

CIPOLLA, C. M., *Cristofano and the Plague*, Berkeley-London, 1973.

CIPOLLA, C. M., *Public Health and the Medical Profession in the Renaissance*, Cambridge, 1976.

COCHRANE, E., *Florence in the forgotten centuries 1527–1800*, Chicago-London, 1973.

CONSOLI FIEGO, G., *Peste e carestie in Pistoia*, Pistoia, 1920.

CORRADI, A., *Annali delle epidemie occorse in Italia dalle prime memorie fino al 1850*, Bologna, 1867–72.

DE ROBERTIS, A., 'Nuovi particolari sulla peste del 1630 in Firenze', in *Memorie Dominicane* 64. 1947.

DIAZ, F., *Il Granducato di Toscana*, Turin, 1976.

FONTANI, F., *Viaggio pittorico della Toscana*, Florence, 1801.

GALLUZZI, R., *Istoria del Granducato di Toscana sotto il Gorverno della Casa Medici*, Florence, 1781.

LANGLET, J. C. N., *Un Bureau de Santé au XVII siècle*, Reims, 1898.

RIGHI, A., *Historia contagiosi morbi qui Florentiam depopulatus est anno 1630*, Florence, 1633.

RONDINELLI, F., *Relazione del contagio stato in Firenze l'anno 1630 e 1633*, Florence, 1634.

Notes

Chapter 1

1 Antero M. San Bonaventura, *Li Lazzaretti*. In this as in the following notes citations are given in an abbreviated form. For full bibliographical references, see Bibliography at the end of the book.

2 Rondinelli, *Relazione*, p. 82.

3 Canon Cini's objectivity, for example, is proved by his report of 7 June 1633, concerning 'a large riot with danger of armed violence' that occurred in San Gimignano over health matters : the good canon did not hesitate to report that 'the riot was provoked, encouraged and spread by priests' (ASF Sanità, Negozi, b. 169, c. 113). ASF is used in the notes for Archivio di Stato, Florence.

4 ASF Sanità, Partiti, b. 10, c. 92.

5 For an account of the whole story see Battistini, *Le epidemie,* pp. 35–7.

6 Consoli Fiego, *Peste e Carestie,* p. 94, n. 3.

7 Galluzzi, *Istoria del Granducato,* Vol. 3, p. 454.

8 The ordinance dated 20 May 1633 was issued for the occasion of the procession of the miraculous image of the *Impruneta* when the Health Magistracy of Florence sought to limit the influx of people to the procession : cf. ASF Sanità, Negozi, b. 168, c. 992.

In Tuscany, as in the rest of the Italian peninsula, the majority of those taking part in religious ceremonies were women and children, and it is indicative of the practical good sense of the contemporary health officials that in seeking a compromise between religious demands and sanitary precautions, they were particularly concerned with preventing the assembly of women and children on the occasion of processions and similar ceremonies. See, for example, the edict of 12 June 1631 (ASF Sanità, Negozi, b. 158, c. 679).

9 For example, in November 1630, the Health Magistracy in

Florence prohibited by public edict 'the holding of schools in the city of Florence, forbidding not only teachers to hold them but also fathers, mothers or other relatives to send their children to school.' (ASF Sanità, Rescritti, b. 37, c. 593 and Sanità, Negozi, b. 152, c. 917).

10 In November 1630 the Magistracy proclaimed 'that gambling houses should be closed and gatherings for games, whether legal or illegal, should not be held, whether in houses or shops.' Cf. ASF Sanità, Rescritti, b. 37, c. 590 and c. 991 and Sanità, Negozi, b. 152, c. 917.

11 See, for instance, the case quoted in Langlet, *Un Bureau de Santé au XVII siècle*, pp. 122–34.

12 For the story of the procession of St Antonio cf. De Robertis, *Nuovi particolari sulla peste*, pp. 166ff.; Catellacci, *Curiosi ricordi*, p. 386; Rondinelli, *Relazione*, pp. 93–94.

Chapter 2
1 On the origins and development of Public Health in Italy between the XVth and XVIIth centuries cf. Cipolla, *Public Health*, Part 1.

Chapter 3
1 Fontani, *Viaggio Pittorico della Toscana*, Vol. 2, p. 134.
2 *ibid.*
3 Inside the castello limits 102 families with a total of 469 inhabitants were counted in 1552, and 131 families with 562 inhabitants in 1562. The whole district (Podesteria), including the neighbouring village of Lastra, had 5,890 inhabitants in 1562 and 5,891 in 1662 (BNF Magliab. II, I, 120 and 240; ASF Misc Medicea 224). BNF is used in the notes for Biblioteca Nazionale, Florence.
4 For the opinions of Father Dragoni, Mayor della Stufa, and the surgeon, Coveri concerning the Monte Lupans cf. respectively ASF Sanità, Negozi, b. 155, c. 365 (11 Feb. 1631); b. 157, c. 560 (18 May 1631) and c. 672 (21 May 1631).
5 The report from the town of Empoli is preserved in ASF Sanità, Negozi, b. 151, c. 242 (5 Oct. 1630). For the parish register of the dead in Monte Lupo, cf. Appendix 3.
6 See Archivio Comunale di Monte Lupo, Saldi antichi.
7 For Father Dragoni's age cf. ASF Sanità, Negozi, b. 154, c. 435 (10 Jan. 1631). For his opinion of local priests, cf. below pp. 56, 83.

For his preaching activity cf. ASF Sanità, Partiti, b. 9, c. 186 (26 March 1632).

8 ASF Sanità, Negozi, b. 154, c. 435 (10 Jan. 1631).

9 E.g. a declaration of 23 Feb. and another of 25 Mar. 1631, were signed by Father Dragoni and five deputies. However the notary signed for one of the deputies because that deputy 'said he did not know how to write.' ASF Sanità, Negozi, b. 155, c. 736, and b. 156, c. 9.

10 Cf. Appendix 3.

11 ASF Sanità, Negozi, b. 152, c. 737.

12 For the number of patients admitted to the opening of the pest-house cf. ASF Sanità, Negozi, b. 152, c. 689. For the number present on 22 October, Appendix 3.

13 For all the preceding, cf. ASF Sanità, Negozi, b. 152, c. 372 (8 Nov. 1630), c. 689 (15 Nov. 1630); b. 153, c. 837 (16 Dec. 1630), c. 950 (19 Dec. 1630) and Sanità, Copialettere, b. 56, c. 94 (19 Dec. 1630).

14 ASF Sanità, Negozi, b. 153, c. 986 (20 Dec. 1630).

15 ASF Sanità, Negozi, b. 153, c. 986 (20 Dec. 1630).

16 For all details of the thefts, inquiries, and arrests, cf. ASF Sanità, Negozi, b. 153, c. 1158 (26 Dec. 1630) and b. 154, c. 123 (3 Jan. 1631).

17 For details of above, cf. ASF Sanità, Negozi, b. 154, c. 435 (10 Jan. 1631), and c. 511 (12 Jan. 1631).

18 ASF Copialettere, b. 56, c. 144 (15 Jan. 1631).

19 ASF Sanità, Negozi, b. 155, c. 13 (1 Feb. 1631).

20 *Ibid.*

21 ASF Sanità, Negozi, b. 155, c. 11 and c. 13 (1 Feb. 1631).

22 ASF Sanità, Negozi, b. 154, c. 796 (18 Jan. 1631).

23 ASF Sanità, Negozi, b. 154, c. 931 (22 Jan. 1631).

24 ASF Sanità, Negozi, b. 155, c. 365 (11 Feb. 1631).

25 ASF Sanità, Rescritti, b. 37, c. 816 (21 Feb. 1631).

26 ASF Sanità, Negozi, b. 154, c. 932 (22 Jan. 1631).

27 ASF Sanità, Rescritti, b. 37, c. 816 (21 Feb. 1631).

28 Rescript on a letter of 22 Jan. 1631, in ASF Sanità, Negozi, b. 154, c. 932.

29 ASF Sanità, Negozi, b. 155, c. 360 (11 Feb. 1631).

30 ASF Sanità, Rescritti, b. 37, c. 816 (21 Feb. 1631).

31 ASF Sanità, Negozi, b. 155, c. 1270 (13 March 1631).

32 ASF Sanità, Negozi, b. 155, c. 1293 (14 March 1631).

33 ASF Sanità, Partiti, b. 4, c. 110v (19 March 1631). The letter communicating to Monte Lupo the decision of 19 March was written on 21 March (ASF Sanità, Copialettere, b. 156, c. 9).

34 ASF Sanità, Negozi, b. 156, c. 9 (25 March 1631).

35 ASF Sanità, Negozi, b. 154, c. 435 (10 Jan. 1631).

36 ASF Sanità, Negozi, b. 156, c. 88 (27 March 1631).

37 ASF Sanità, Negozi Copialettere, b. 57, c. 49.

38 ASF Sanità, Negozi, b. 156, c. 201 (1 April 1631).

39 ASF Sanità, Copialettere, b. 57, c. 56 (4 April 1631).

40 ASF Sanità, Copialettere, b. 57, cc 73 and 78.

41 The Mayor's age is established by the parish book of the dead for Monte Lupo. Cf. Appendix 3.

42 ASF Sanità, Negozi, b. 156, c. 637 (16 April 1631).

43 ASF Sanità, Negozi, b. 156, c. 694 (19 April 1631). Cf. also b. 157, c. 123 (5 May 1631).

44 Rescript on a letter in ASF Sanità, Negozi, b. 156, c. 694.

45 For all of the preceding, cf. ASF Sanità, Negozi, b. 157, c. 9 (1 May 1631), and c. 123 (5 May 1631); Sanità, Copialettere, b. 57, c. 94 (2 May 1631).

46 ASF Sanità, Copialettere, b. 57, c. 104 (10 May 1631).

47 ASF Sanità, Negozi, b. 157, c. 398 (12 May 1631).

48 ASF Sanità, Copialettere, b. 57, c. 109 (13 May 1631).

49 ASF Sanità, Negozi, b. 157, c. 560 (18 May 1631).

50 ASF Sanità, Negozi, b. 156, c. 988 (29 April 1631).

51 ASF Sanità, Negozi, b. 157, c. 9 (1 May 1631).

52 ASF Sanità, Negozi, b. 157, c. 560 (18 May 1631).

53 Cf. Appendix 3.

54 Consequently the letter is erroneously filed in the Public Health archives under the month of May: ASF Sanità, Negozi, b. 157, c. 99.

55 ASF Sanità, Copialettere, b. 57, c. 159.

56 ASF Sanità, Negozi, b. 158, c. 199 (6 June 1631).

57 Sanità, Copialettere, b. 57, c. 134v (24 May 1631).

58 ASF Sanità, Copialettere, b. 57, c. 168 (6 June 1631).

59 ASF Sanità, Copialettere, b. 57, c. 178v (9 June 1631).

60 ASF Sanità, Negozi, b. 158, c. 117 (28 June 1631).

61 ASF Sanità, Negozi, b. 158, c. 117 (28 June 1631).
62 ASF Sanità, Negozi, b. 159, cc. 672 and 878.
63 ASF Sanità, Negozi, b. 159, c. 734 (22 July 1631).
64 ASF Sanità, Negozi, b. 159, cc. 762ff., 836ff.
65 ASF Sanità, Negozi, b. 160, c. 630 (23 Aug. 1631).
66 When separate archival references are not given in the pages that follow, this means that the information reported is taken from the sources indicated in the three preceding notes.

Chapter 4
1 On the right hand wall of the church of the convent of St. Marco in Florence, between the second and third altars, under the pulpit, is a tombstone which reads :

D.O.M.
MEMORIAE
FR. BENEDICTI SACCHETTI EQUITI HIEROSOLIMITANI
QUI MAIORUM SUORUM LAUDES
ORDINISQUE NOBILISSIMI GLORIAM
REBUS FORTITER GESTIS MARITIMIS PRESERTIM
ADVERSUS CHRISTIANI NOMINI HOSTES
EXPEDITIONIS CUMULAVIT
PIA GENTILIUM CURA
HOC POSITO MONUMENTO CONSULUIT
OBIIT KAL OCTOBRIS CIƆ IƆC XXXII
AETATIS SUAE ANNORUM XLVIIII

2 ASF Sanità, Negozi, b. 159, c. 847 (25 July 1631).
3 ASF Sanità, Negozi, b. 155, c. 897 (28 Feb. 1631).
4 ASF Sanità, Rescritti, b. 37, c. 178 (19 Aug. 1630).
5 ASF Sanità, Negozi, b. 158, c. 880 (23 June 1631).
6 Cipolla, *Cristofano and the Plague*, p. 54.
7 ASF Sanità, Negozi, b. 168, c. 1025 (2 May 1633).
8 ASF Sanità, Negozi, b. 157, c. 672 (21 May 1631).
9 Cipolla, *Cristofano and the Plague*, p. 54, n. 3.
10 ASF Partiti, b. 4, c. 86 (30 Jan. 1631).
11 This hypothesis is corroborated by the fact that on 28 February, Coveri asked the Health Magistracy for a certificate of satisfactory service (ASF Sanità, Negozi, b. 155, c. 897).

12 ASF Sanità, Negozi, b. 155, c. 897 (28 Feb. 1631) and b. 157, c. 672 (21 May 1631).

13 ASF Sanità, Partiti, b. 4, c. 100 (1 March 1631).

14 ASF Sanità, Partiti, b. 10, c. 117v (18 Dec. 1632).

15 ASF Sanità, Partiti, c. 126v (18 Jan. 1633).

16 ASF Sanità, Negozi, b. 157, c. 672 (21 May 1631).

17 As specified above (p. 49, n. 6), all details regarding the processions and interrogations in Monte Lupo are taken from the sources cited in the notes 63, 64, 65 of Chapter 3.

18 ASF Sanità, Negozi, b. 159, c. 582 (17 July 1631).

19 Don Bontadi's age at the time of the events in Monte Lupo is derived from the parish book of the dead for the Castello. See p. 99. above.

20 See Archivio Comunale di Monte Lupo, Saldi antichi, filza 61/G c. 49 r.

21 ASF Sanità, Negozi, b. 159, c. 735 (22 July 1631).

22 ASF Sanità, Negozi, b. 159, c. 847 (25 July 1631).

23 ASF Sanità, Negozi, b. 159, c. 916 (27 July 1631).

24 ASF Sanità, Negozi, b. 160, c. 166 (8 Aug. 1631).

Chapter 5

1 ASF Sanità, Negozi, b. 159, cc. 693, 731.

2 ASF Sanità, Negozi, b. 159, c 673 (15 Aug. 1631).

3 On 3 August, Simone da Schifanoia fell ill; his name appears on the list of those who took part in the procession. Five days earlier Sandra di Polidoro had fallen sick. She does not appear specifically on the list, but there is a Camillo di Polidoro 'with another member of the family', so it is possible that Sandra was that other member.

Chapter 6

1 ASF Sanità, Negozi, b. 162, c. 197, and ibid., b. 160, c. 55.

2 The information about Father Dragoni's tribulations described above is drawn from ASF Sanità, Negozi, b. 160, c. 269 (11 Aug. 1631), 634 and 848 (23 Aug. 1631); b. 161, c. 45 (2 Sept. 1631), and c. 424 (12 Sept. 1631); b. 162, c. 197 (8 Oct. 1631).

3 ASF Sanità, Negozi, b. 162, c. 749 (27 Oct. 1631), and ASF Sanità, Partiti, b. 9, c. 113v.

4 ASF Sanità, Negozi, b. 163, c. 117 (7 Nov. 1631).

5 *Ibid*.

6 ASF Sanità, Negozi, b. 163, c. 567 (26 Nov. 1631).

7 Cf. the *Libro dei Morti* for Monte Lupo, for which see App. 3.

8 See note 1 of Chapter 4.